MW01232737

FLORIDA PIONEER
TO LAND BARON

FLORIDA PIONEER TO LAND BARON

How to Make A Fortune in Florida Real Estate

JACK FREEMAN

CONTENTS

PROLOGUE

This book is really about Florida's growth from 1950 through 2003, and how the vast untapped jungles of sun-drenched lands were developed and sold to a public that had gone through a depression and a world war, a public that was tired of all the sacrifices, a public that was fully employed cranking out products not available during the war, a public with disposable income looking for an easier way of life. They wanted a place where the sun shone year-round; where the pace of living was slower; where they could retire when they completed their mandatory work hitched to the industrial machines. Florida was the ideal place—the best fishing in the world, the finest beaches, year-round sun, easy laid-back living. However, people were wary of the word "Florida." All the popular conceptions of the state were based on unhappy stories of the land deals in Florida in the early twentieth century. In that period of time, speculators had bought this jungle land for a few dollars an acre, never having seen the land, but with a drawing board, in Chicago, Cleveland or New York, they divided the land into hundreds of "plats" which were filed in the county courthouses. Much of this land actually was "swamp land." Therefore, "Florida Swamp Land" became equivalent to the expression "buying the Brooklyn Bridge." Even today, in the public records of many Florida counties, you can still find old, now outdated, plats filed in the twenties.

Everyone was aware of the land scandals of the twenties, the thousands of non-existent or unusable lots sold to an unsuspecting public. It was known as the Florida Land Boom. Predictably, the stuff "hit the fan." In the late twenties, two devastating hurricanes nearly wiped out the nascent cities of Miami and

Miami Beach. Most of South Florida was too marshy to support buildings. While just this news would have been enough to terminate all vestiges of Florida investment, the lurking floodwaters of the national economy also burst, the stock market crashed, and the whole country went bankrupt. There were few jobs; many people had no money, even for food. There were soup kitchens in every city; people sold apples on the street corners; the banks were closed. Everyone who had accumulated a small amount of money was wiped out. In 1933 my family had $800 in the Bank of United States in New York. The bank closed. As a boy of thirteen, I waited with my mother for hours in a long line extending around the block. We were all trying to withdraw a few dollars on which to survive.

Thankfully nothing lasts forever. After eleven years of depression, World War II finally put the United States economy back on the road to recovery, and Florida began a new life.

Basically this is the story of two young people, my brother Jules and I, who grew up in the poor ghetto of the Bronx in the early twenties and thirties and who came to Florida in early 1953. We did not realize that we were pioneers. This is the story of how, with just a small amount of money, we were able to build a very successful empire. We started with our first purchase of 240 acres and eventually accumulated, developed, and sold 89,000 acres, or approximately 139 square miles. To put this in context, the entire city of New York comprises 27,000 acres. Therefore we owned and developed properties that were three times the size of New York City. Starting with $10,000, in the twenty years between 1953 and 1973, we built over 200 houses in Miami, built the city of San Carlos Park (where today, over 25,000 people reside); developed several communities in Bonita Springs and Lee County; started, developed and constructed over 30,000 acres of citrus grove, including the largest orange grove in the world; started and developed the pistachio industry in California; and went public in 1968 with our company American Agronomics Corp. After we retired from the company in 1973, we continued dealing in Florida real estate, developing and selling properties and citrus groves, for our families, and ourselves until the present time.

It is important to understand that in the early nineteen-fifties Florida's economy was still in a disastrous condition. Air conditioning was unknown; the land was considered a swamp; and above all, only a few local banks with limited funds were available for investment loans. The few developers who started to build and develop could not obtain money from the local banks; they had no money to lend. The moneyed northern banks in New York, Chicago, etc., refused to lend money in Florida. I remember that Jay Kislak, a friend and neighbor of mine who owned a very large and respected mortgage company in New Jersey, opened an office in Miami to supply mortgage monies to builders. The big northern banks that lent him large sums of money for New Jersey, refused to lend him money for Florida. He spent a great deal of money, effort, and time, flying these bankers down to Miami, taking them on fishing trips, wining and dining them to obtain some financial commitments to maintain the budding building industry.

As Dickens aptly put it, "It was the best of times; it was the worst of times." Those who didn't have money had to work hard and stretch every dollar. It was in this unsettling situation that I arrived in Florida in 1953. My brother and I researched the Florida economy at that time. The population of the state was under 4,000,000 people. In 2003, there are now more than 16,000,000 in Florida. Prior to 1953 there were just two ways to get to Florida: either people drove or came by airplane. Driving from the typical city up north took at least three full days, mostly over two-lane dangerous roads. By air, in the state-of-the-art four-engine propeller plane, the trip took 6 to 7 hours.

One of the prime reasons we were bullish on Florida was that the airlines were just preparing to receive the new four-engine jet planes. On these planes the trip to Florida would take only three hours and make this state a prime vacation area. I envisioned people living in New York, owning an apartment or home in Florida and spending Monday through Thursday working in New York, and Friday to Sunday in sunny Florida. It appeared only a matter of time before Florida would come into its own as one of the most desirable places in the world to live.

To acquaint the reader with a sense of the growth that

occurred in the development of the state, as the Bible says "In the Beginning", I include a short history of Florida, focusing mainly on its economic and growth factors.

I want to give special thanks to my niece and nephew, Myrna and Ronnie Wohl, who were kind enough to read the first draft of this book. They gave me encouragement and helpful suggestions for corrections and additions to my work. Thanks also to Dr.Priscilla Van Zandt, who edited my final draft.

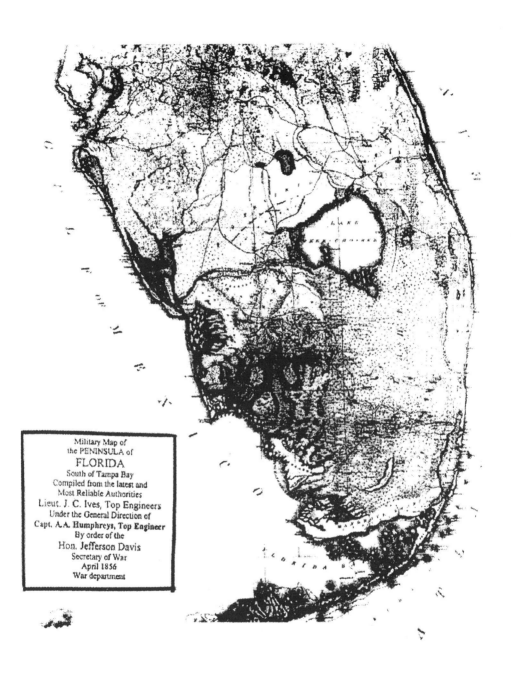

This is a map of Florida as it was in 1856.
(The darker areas were too marshy to build on)

CHAPTER ONE

HISTORY OF FLORIDA

The State of Florida is unique in the United States. Stretching from south to north over 400 miles, it is the only state in the union that has truly tropical weather. It is also a state with almost no mountains but with hundreds of miles of beach and waterfront on both the Atlantic Ocean and the Gulf of Mexico. It has one of the largest lakes in the world, Lake Okeechobee, and hundreds of miles of riverfront on the St. Johns River, the famed Suwanee River, the Caloosahatchee River, and many others.

Florida is a state of endless blessings: a wonderful, mild climate, almost constant sunshine and the best beaches in the world. It is truly a paradise. Furthermore, it is blessed with plentiful water resources that make the state ideal for agriculture. For example, California gets an average rainfall of 12 inches per year, while Florida gets an average rainfall of 57 inches. Therefore, it is no wonder that in winter when most of the northern states are snow-bound and freezing, Florida sends fruits and vegetables northward. Also, though it is not generally known, Florida is the second largest cattle state in the country, after Texas. Florida is known as the "Winter Breadbasket of the North."

Fortunately for all mankind, when the first pioneers came to the United States they were essentially fleeing from the "Old World" to the "New World." They were escaping from religious and political persecution in Europe, a continent for thousands of years beset by intermittent warfare, each country trying to conquer the neighboring state; constantly trying to enforce their politics or religion on their neighbors. Therefore the pioneers who came to this country started with a clean book. They could compose their lives and fortunes without interference from hostile neighbors. No one could tell them how or where to work, where to live, or how to worship. That is how freedom was born in this U.S.A.

Explorers from European countries were the first discoverers of Florida. Because all of these countries were constantly at war with each other, the nationalities of the explorers who crossed the ocean varied from time to time depending on which country were in ascendancy at that time. First came the Spaniards. Juan Ponce de Leon reached Florida in April 1513, probably around the area of St. Augustine. He called this new land "Florida" in honor of the "feast of flowers" in Spain. Hernando De Soto, also a Spaniard, came to Florida in 1521 and traveled throughout the state looking for gold and other treasures to loot from the few native Indians.

In 1562 and subsequent years, the French explorers, Jean Ribault and Rene de Laudonniere established a fort near Jacksonville. Spain, not to be outdone, sent another explorer, Pedro Menendez de Aviles, who arrived at St.Augustine in 1565, set up the first European settlement in Florida, and expelled the French settlers in the area. The French responded several years later by murdering the Spanish soldiers. As the English became more powerful and replaced Spain as the dominant power in Europe, the English settlers arrived in Virginia and Plymouth in years 1607 and 1620. They eventually pushed south as far as Florida and replaced the Spaniards who had become dominant in the state. Spain relinquished political power but did not finally cede the state to the United States until 1821, in a formal treaty known as the Adams-Onis Treaty.

In 1821, General Andrew Jackson established a territorial government in Florida on behalf of the United States. A state capital was established in the new city of Tallahassee in 1824. Settlers who had migrated from northern cities, escaped slaves, and native Indians—primarily Creek and Miccosukee people, populated the state. The United States government wanted to eliminate the Indians and there ensued many Seminole Wars aimed at "liquidating" the native Indians. As that became impossible, because the Indians were excellent fighters, the government captured some, and sent them westward. However, many Seminoles resisted and escaped into the Everglades. They still live there today in Immokalee, Hollywood, Okeechobee, and along the Big Cypress Swamp.

By 1840, the population of Florida had reached 54,477. One-half of the population was African-American slaves. The balance was white Floridians who had migrated from northern areas. On March 3, 1845, Florida became the twenty-seventh state in the union. William D. Moseley was elected the new state's first governor. By 1850, the population had grown to 87,445 people. When the Civil War began in 1861, Florida sided with the southern states and seceded from the Union.

After the Civil War, Florida's main economic development centered on large-scale agriculture and cattle raising. Florida's climate was ideal for cattle. Cows could graze the year-round on the plentiful grass. As a result, the state became number one in what is known as a "cow-calf" operation. In other words, even at the present time, cattle are raised in Florida for the "calf" crop. The cows are then shipped out west to the "corn belt" for feeding and eventual slaughter. In the latter part of the nineteenth century, citrus was introduced to the state, and orange and grapefruit groves were intensively developed, providing fruit for the northern markets.

However, cattle raising became an enormous industry, and vast herds roamed the state. There were numerous "cattle wars" when competing cattle barons vied for the open pasture. Sometime the herds were driven hundreds of miles, ranging from Tampa to Miami, in search of available grass. It was exactly like the Wild West we see in the movies—cattle barons and cowboys driving herds of cattle long distances and engaging in constant feuds between the competing cattlemen. Florida was at that time an open range, a "no fence" state. Because of the clout and importance of the cattlemen and their political power, it was illegal to fence any property. The cows were first priority and they could not be contained.

In the early 1950s, when Fuller Warren was governor,

Florida's population had increased to the extent that the free roaming cows were a threat to both people and vehicles. Despite great opposition from the cattlemen, Governor Warren courageously enacted "fence" legislation that required all cattle ranches to be fenced. Incidentally, Fuller Warren was a great person and admirable politician. I knew him as a friend. When we went public with our company, American Agronomics Corp., in 1968, we appointed Fuller to our Board of Directors.

A map of Florida in the mid-nineteenth century showed very few roads, mostly just cattle trails. The most startling thing you would notice was that the land south of a line between Tampa and Vero Beach was all "swamp." Much land south of that line was a wet marsh. It became imperative to "drain the swamp." Accordingly in the 1870s, the Governor entered into a contract of sale wherein the State of Florida sold over three million acres, at 50 cents per acre—essentially the entire southern part of the state—to Henry Disston, a wealthy northern entrepreneur. Disston was a Philadelphia tool manufacturer, famous for having invented and perfected the "Disston Saw." Even today carpenters buy only Disston saws because of their superiority. As part of the purchase deal with the State of Florida, Disston was obligated to "drain the swamp."

Disston used the primitive earth-moving equipment available at that time and drained the land by building a large canal and channeling the standing water into Lake Okeechobee. The project was huge and costly, almost impossible to accomplish with the machines available at that time. While Disston accomplished much, he was unable to complete the drainage job. He went bankrupt and the state reclaimed the entire southern part of the state. Most of the transportation at that time was by boat, since there were almost no roads. Beginning in the late nineteenth century and early twentieth century, many rich northern merchants and businessmen became aware of Florida, its beautiful climate, beaches, and sunshine. They started to "winter" in the Sunshine State. In 1855, the state had passed an Internal Improvement Act, offering cheap or free land to any person who would build transportation facilities. Taking advantage of this situation, Henry Flagler and

Henry B. Plant, both rich Northern industrialists, built railroads from Jacksonville to Miami and eventually to Key West, and from Tampa east to St. Augustine. They also built lavish hotels near their railroad lines to house the expected tourists.

Eventually more roads were constructed from Georgia southward. While the roads were primitive and scarce, as automobiles came into production in the early twentieth century, it finally became possible to travel to Florida by auto. Therefore, in the years 1920-1926, Florida became a boom state. Florida land was being sold all over the country. So-called "developers" purchased thousands of acres. Typically, these individuals purchased land, sight unseen, for a few dollars an acre, drew up a map subdividing the acreage into lots, and filed these maps in the county registers. They sold countless thousands of lots and acres. It was an enormous marketing feat, accomplished with newspaper advertising, soft-shoe land salesmen, marketing offices in the North or in Florida. Even that most famous politician and orator, William Jennings Bryant, became a spokesman for land developers touting the value of Florida land.

As in all human endeavors, time and events change. A devastating hurricane hit Florida in 1926 and almost destroyed even the sparsely populated city areas. As the hurricane moved through Miami westward, it caused Lake Okeechobee to overflow. Three thousand people were drowned as the lake ran out of its bank into the surrounding farms and homes, in the cities of Clewiston and Moore Haven. Florida's growth came to a devastating halt. The worst result was that Florida land became a matter of derision. No sane person would then invest in the state. Sale of Florida land was placed in the same category as "buying the Brooklyn Bridge." Of course, the stock market crash in 1929 and the subsequent depression sounded the death knell to all investments in the country—both business and real estate.

The depression devastated the entire world economy. Between 1929 and 1941, there was widespread poverty throughout the country. With the entry of the U.S. into World War II, the U.S.A. went all-out to defeat the Axis countries, Japan and Germany.

The country entered on a complete war footing. All auto plants and factories were converted to war production. These factories eventually produced tanks, ships and airplanes by the thousands in an unbelievable spurt of the country's industrial might. In Florida, because of its year-round mild climate, airports were constructed all over the state. Soldiers and airmen were stationed in many of the cities. The hotels in Miami and in other Florida cities were converted into lodgings for the hordes of soldiers being trained. After the war, many of the discharged soldiers preferred to remain in the state rather than return to their northern homes.

As time passed, more and more people visited Florida, vacationing in Miami and other cities, swimming in the sun-drenched oceans, lying on the clean sandy beaches and enjoying a good vacation. Auto production had been suspended during the war, but now, for the first time in years, people could buy automobiles. And where did you go when you got your new auto and went on vacation? Naturally, Florida! Thus started a complete new chapter in the economic growth of Florida.

Jack Freeman (1970)

CHAPTER TWO

PERSONAL HISTORY

As, I write this, I am 83 years old. I was born in 1919 in a completely different world than exists today. My parents were immigrants who had come to this country in the vast European exodus in the 1890-1920 period. The people who were lucky enough to escape from Europe to the "new land" came here with tremendous energy and a desire to succeed. My parents were Jews who came from a little town in Poland called Belchatov. The whole town had about 11,500 people. Of this total, 11,000 inhabitants were Jews. During the "holocaust" almost the entire Jewish population was exterminated.

Fortunately for my parents, my mother's cousin had emigrated from this little town in the 1870s, had come to America and had, over time, built a very large clothing manufacturing business—one of the largest in the world at that time. His business was R. Sadowski & Co. He had many manufacturing plants in the New York area and employed hundreds of seamstresses. Since he needed workers for these factories to operate the sewing machines, he imported many of his relatives from Belchatov and brought them to America. My grandfather was R. Sadowski's uncle. And thus, in 1905, my grandfather and grandmother (on my mother's side), together with their eight children, came to this country and were immediately employed in the factory. My father also emigrated at the same time. My mother and father had known each other from the old country, so they began dating and were married in 1909.

My father was a bright man and a wonderful businessman. In Belchatov, my grandmother (on my father's side) was in business operating what we today would call a "paint store." It wasn't really paint because, at that time, there was no paint. She sold whitewash, which was used to paint the houses. My grandmother was a good business lady and her store was profitable. Her husband, my grandfather, was a scholar. He spent his time studying and reading the Bible, attending the synagogue and helping run the business when necessary. They had a little piece of land, grew vegetables, and had a horse and wagon for traveling to the big city of Lodz, some 28 miles away. Every morning the horse and wagon would make the trip to take passengers to and from the city, returning with bags of whitewash for the store. From the time that my father was ten years old, his job was taking care of the horse and wagon, driving the rig every morning to the big city, taking any passengers who required transportation and loading and returning with the bags of whitewash and other materials necessary for the store. He was about eighteen years old before he received permission to emigrate to America. He was immediately recruited to work in the "sweatshop" factories in New York.

My father was a brilliant man and very good at business. It was not long before he saved enough money to start his own business. In 1915, he and his brother-in-law opened a retail store downtown on Second Avenue and Eighth Street. They manufactured and sold women's cloaks and suits. In the rear of the store, seamstresses worked at six or seven machines, producing suits and coats for the ladies. Over a period of time, they had a large stock of clothing on display. At that time when there were no department stores, it was customary for a woman to go to the store for a coat or suit and have her measurements taken. The garment was then made to order for her, to be delivered in one week. The business was very successful. As the city grew and people started to move from the ghettos of the Lower East Side "uptown," my father opened another store on 125th Street, in Harlem. At that time many well-to-do citizens lived in Harlem, on the north side of Central Park, and these were basically the customers who patronized my father's store.

I was born in 1919 in an apartment above my father's store on Second Avenue. This area was known as the "Lower East Side." It was an area full of with immigrants from the old country. A large majority of the population were Jews, but there were also many Italians, Irishmen, and other refugees trying to fit into the American mainstream.

They were hard workers. Many were people of great talent and ability who needed only the American freedom to express their ability and enrich themselves and also this wonderful country. Hundreds of musicians, performers, business people, scholars, judges, politicians, etc. came from these congested tenement houses. The best of American music came from the Gershwins, Irving Berlin, and other noted musicians—all graduates of the Lower East Side school. It was also inevitable that in this crowded populous area, the Mafia developed, and some of our most notorious gangsters were spawned here.

As the city of New York expanded northward, away from the teeming streets of the Lower East Side, people started to move up to Harlem and further north to the Bronx.

In 1925, when I was six years old, my parents moved to an apartment in the Bronx, a completely new setting. At that time, there were almost no individual homes. The entire Bronx consisted of multi-floor apartment buildings. There were no elevators. We walked up and down the stairs to get to our apartment. The good side to living in this environment was that children automatically had hundreds of companions, and there were always countless activities going on. Going up and down the stairs in the apartment building, kids were playing cards on the steps; in the streets, there were "stick ball" games; kids were playing marbles; kids were fighting or playing various athletic games.

At the bottom of the basement stairs of an apartment, sometimes a crap game would spring up. Nickels and dimes flew from hand to pavement. Starting with three kids, the number might swell to ten or more. The winners picked up their money and continued. Some players faded away as they went broke. They played until the winners picked up their money, or they dispersed when someone yelled, "Chickee the Cops." These untutored kids displayed more mathematical skill than some professor of mathematics—all without the benefit of an education.

Further up the block a group of three teens might be having a heated discussion, and using chalk to diagram their exciting discoveries. These were devotees of science. They are oblivious to the ball games. Their prime interest was in science, chemistry, and physics. They wanted to discover amazing things to revolutionize human existence. One kid I knew, who later became a prominent physician, unbelievably got his kicks and honed his technique by dissecting dead cats.

As I look at today's families, I see mothers and fathers creating all types of activities to keep their kids occupied— soccer games, vacations, trips, etc. I think we were better off in those times. All our fathers were working hard trying to eke out a living for their families. The kids all occupied themselves in their own way. And it was great! We had many choices. We could choose our own friends from the hundreds of kids on the block. Many kids played ball. Some played the harmonica and others sang along. There were all kinds of kids from whom to choose friends. There were low class kids, intelligent kids, aggressive kids, etc. Some of us would walk along, singing the popular songs of the day. There was one kid, Philly Lebowitz, who had a terrible ear for music. Since he was a good friend of ours, my brother spent hours teaching him how to sing. Many years later Philly went into show business and become a very successful actor. He won the Amateur Hour, was bitten by the acting bug, changed his name to Phil Leeds, and became a prominent star with Sid Caesar on the first television programs, co-starred in Cole Porter's "Can-Can" on Broadway, went on to Hollywood where he became a character actor in many films.

Most families were living on the edge of poverty, but we, as kids, did not know it. We also did not know that we were all enrolled in the best college in the world. We were learning things that no Harvard or Yale graduate ever learns. We were going to the "Hard-Knocks" University. The main course was "Survival 101". We had to learn how to handle the good kids, the bullies, and the gangs, and we had to survive. We had no one to complain to; no one to take care of our problems. If we couldn't handle them, we were in trouble. Every other kid knew us, and how we reacted. In this environment we quickly learned many rules: Avoid controversy; think of different ways to handle each situation; be ahead of the curve; watch your behind; stand up to bullies; pick your battles—on your own turf; use your knowledge; evaluate your competitor, beat him by making him play your game. These and many other stratagems we had to learn in order to survive. For example, when I was about 10 years old, one schoolyard bully was picking on and beating some of my friends. Once he started to accost me, and I knew that it was time to "sink or swim." His name was, believe it or not, John Battle. We arranged to have one big fight to settle this matter—at lunchtime, out on the street behind the school. As half of the school kids watched, John Battle and I went at it, with fists flying. After a few moments, with some slight physical damage to each combatant, we decided to stop the fight. As I recall, no one won decisively. All I know was, from that time on, John Battle respected me and never again bothered me or my friends.

As a kid growing up in this environment, I had many choices. Most of the kids were into athletics, ball playing, games, etc. I was not athletic, and did not enjoy athletic pursuits. I was into reading, learning, and mental gymnastics. I would walk miles to the public library, take out three or four books, read them, return them a few days later and check out more books to read. My father bought an encyclopedia called the *Book of Knowledge*. There were twenty books in this set, and I read those thousand pages over and over, becoming familiar with the history, workings and knowledge of mankind.

Every family in those days had a piano in the living room, and it was not uncommon to see pianos hoisted up to the apartments through the windows or being lowered as people moved to other apartments. Generally, these newly Americanized people were persons of culture. Their daughters invariably were encouraged to play the piano; the sons were invariably made to play the violin, some willingly and some under duress. No family had money but everyone had some intellectual interests and "culture."

This was the era of Prohibition. It was not unusual for some of the people to make their own whiskey in bathtubs. Some people even made money selling this alcohol. Of course, there was no television. Radio was just becoming popular. My parents bought our first radio in 1928. It cost around $700.00, a gigantic amount of money at that time. The stores that sold radios usually played the radios through loud speakers outside their stores to encourage sales. Most people could not afford the purchase price, so they would stand outside the stores, listening. If there was a world championship boxing match, or other public event, huge crowds could be seen on the sidewalks outside the radio stores listening to a report of the action.

When I was six years old and my family had just moved to the Bronx, I started school at P.S. 42. I was a good student. Every day my mother packed a sandwich and a drink for me, and that was lunch. I walked to and from school—several miles. However, since most of the kids came from poor families, it did not take long for us to realize that the only way out of this ghetto was through acquiring a good education. Our parents were also urging us to perform. Most of the teachers at that time were very good. Teaching was a respected profession, and teachers were disciplinarians. If students were rowdy or disruptive, they were sent to the principal's office. It did not take long for students to know that they had to behave. If they did not behave, punishment was meted out in several different ways. Usually the teacher hit them in the behind with a ruler, or they sat in front of the room wearing a "dunce cap," but this was only the beginning.

The worst punishment was that the teacher notified the student's parents. When the student returned home, I need not describe the beatings and other punishments, mental and physical, administered by the parents.

So all the ingredients for a good education existed at that time. We were poor but we had a wonderful, loving family. In retrospect, I think we had good genes. As I write this, my sister Sylvia is 93 years old, my brother Jules is 89, and I am 83. While I was in grade school, my brother Jules, would teach me subjects that he was taking. For example, while I was in the sixth grade, Jules would teach me French. So when I finally started French in the seventh grade, I was way ahead of the other students. My seventh grade teacher was excellent. She worked individually with every child in the class, encouraging all of them, helping and demanding that they learn every subject up to their individual capability. Since I was the brightest kid in the class, the teacher demanded more of me than the others. For example, she knew that I read many books, but she wondered if I read the newspapers, and wanted to know what part I preferred to read. I told her that, in addition to the news, I read the comics—especially Dick Tracy, a very popular comic strip at that time. She asked me if I realized what a waste of time it was, reading the comics. And that started me thinking. I have never since that time ever, ever, wasted my time on comic strips or other unimportant readings.

I spent the seventh through ninth grades in a new school, Herman Ridder Junior High School. This school in the East Bronx was only a few blocks from our apartment building. I was an outstanding student, graduating with highest honors. As the valedictorian, I was awarded the Herman Ridder Gold Medal for excellence—an award which I still have tucked away somewhere in a drawer.

When I was thirteen years old, I was ready for high school. The best high school in New York City at that time was Townsend Harris High School, a special school for bright students. It was a prep school for City College of New York. In other words, students who graduated from Townsend Harris were automatically admitted into City College. City College at that time was a free college run by the State of New York and New York City. Only the brightest students in the city were allowed. Students needed a minimum average grade of 85 to be admitted. City College was the only way a poor kid could go to college at that time during the depression. Almost all of the people in the country were trying to get jobs to earn a meager living. Most families had no money for college; there were no government programs, and no scholarships. Of the few thousand students who applied to Townsend Harris, only between 300-400 per year were accepted. All applicants had to take a three day difficult examination. I was sure that I would not get in. However, I was pleasantly surprised and happy to be admitted.

Townsend Harris was located in the City College Building at Lexington Avenue and 23rd Street. Our "campus" was the elevator since the school was in a thirteen-story building housing the business School of City College. The high school was located in the ninth through eleventh stories of this skyscraper. The schoolrooms were small, approximately 12x15 feet, and housed about twenty students. The professors were all dedicated, superior educators; most were distinguished men in their own fields. They taught there because they knew the students were intelligent and eager to learn. The professors threw the toughest assignments our way. When we started school—in fact the first day—we each were given a list of 100 books that we had to read in three years. The list included works by the greatest writers of all times: Shakespeare, Dickens, and many great English, French and American literary giants. Before graduation, three years later, every student was tested to verify that they had completed these readings. In addition to English courses, we were required to take tough mathematics, and science courses, and two foreign languages.

My high school experience was the finest time of my life. It was very challenging. I awakened each morning at 6 A.M., and had to be at the subway station at 6:30. I lived in the Bronx and the school was in downtown Manhattan. The subway ride took one hour, but of course, the subway fare then (in 1934-1940) was only five cents! School hours were 8AM through 4 PM, with a half hour for lunch. Most of the students would be described as over-achievers! Many students graduated from the high school at the age of fourteen. However there were even some kids who graduated at ten or twelve years of age! I was sixteen. I must mention some graduates from this high school. I don't know how many thousands of students went on to become prominent judges, lawyers, politicians, musicians, professors, dean, doctors, scientists, etc. However, I will mention a few famous graduates: In the field of acting, Edward G. Robinson; in music, Ira Gershwin, Frank Loesser, and Richard Rogers; in literature, Herman Wouk; in science, Dr. Jonas Salk. In fact, Richard Rogers was expelled after his first term because he could not maintain his school grades. He was too busy writing music! Of course, the school later awarded him an honorary diploma.

When I was fifteen years old and in the last year of high school, I hoped to enter college during the next year. There was one problem. No money was available for college or the living expenses I would require for the four college years. It was the depths of the depression in 1935; my father had lost his business, and no jobs were available. The only person in the family with a job was my brother Jules. Fortunately, he had a civil service job with the City of New York. He earned $27.00 per week, and our family of five lived on that salary. Getting a government job at that time was considered extremely desirable. The job was permanent and the pay, though meager, was steady. Jules got the job by taking various civil service examinations. In the newspapers each week, the City of New York would list the jobs available. Since the hiring was done on a merit system, a test was given for each job category. Many of the smarter kids on our street would regularly take these tests just to see how high they came out on the list. It was sort of fun to take the tests; if kids came out near the top of the list when the results were published, it gave them "bragging rights" and enhanced their standing in the street community. Jules had taken one of these tests, and was near the top of the list, and went to work for the city. His $27.00 weekly salary was necessary for the minimum survival of our family, so no funds would be available for me to go to college.

Faced with this problem of finding enough money to attend college, I had to come up with a strategy to accomplish the objective. College tuition was free, since I had the grades to attend the College of the City of New York. What I needed was a part-time job to provide the living expenses during four years of college. Jules and I came up with the solution: I would learn a musical instrument and work my way through college by playing in a band. During the summer recess, I went to work in an Army and Navy store earning $5.00 per week that I contributed to the family coffers. Jules and I saved seven dollars of his salary. In downtown New York, at the Bowery, there was a long line of pawnshops with musical instruments for sale. My instrument of choice was the saxophone. When we found an alto sax in one of the pawnshops, we purchased it for seven dollars.

That saxophone was a great investment. For the next four years, it enabled me to earn enough income to stay in college. I made approximately $450.00 per year, which at that time was sufficient. To learn how to play the sax, I took five lessons. Each lesson cost fifty cents. The sax is an easy instrument to learn, and fortunately I had a very good ear for music. I was going to school with a lot of bright kids. Many of them were already excellent musicians. I had been playing the sax only six months and was really a marginal player at that time. However, I had something that these musical friends of mine did not have—mainly the drive and management ability to assemble a band and find jobs. Accordingly, together with three of my friends, I assembled a four-piece band and circulated around to locate agencies that booked bands, and got us our first job for the summer at a hotel in the Catskill Mountains. The three friends who were in my band were really superior musicians. The violin player, Mel Keller, was a child prodigy, a musical genius. He bought a tenor sax, and in two weeks, without lessons, he was playing the sax like a pro.

At the hotel, besides playing for evening dancing, we usually played "dinner music" for lunch on Sunday. I suggested that Mel play a classical violin piece. He chose Mendelssohn's E Minor Concerto. The guests were astounded to hear this kid, fifteen years old, play such a difficult concerto, usually played only by violinists such as Itzak Perlman or Isaac Stern.

When I enrolled at the City College of New York, I intended to become a doctor, but that was an unrealistic dream. I had no money. Furthermore, at that time, even if one had the money, the medical schools in this country would not accept Jewish students. Jewish students who had the money usually attended overseas schools, received their medical degrees, and then returned to practice. Since becoming a doctor was out of the question, I decided to become an accountant, so I enrolled in the business program at City College. For the next four years, I attended the Baruch School of CCNY at Lexington Avenue and 23rd Street. In the summers, I booked jobs for my band at different hotels in the Catskill Mountains. In the wintertime, at Christmas recess, I would get my band a job at one of the hotels in Lakewood, N.J. During the college year, I played gigs on weekends for weddings, bar mitzvahs, and other affairs. Unbelievably, our compensation on these gigs was $3.00 per musician for four hours of musical play!

When I was twenty years old, about to graduate from college, I was playing with my band at the Alpine Hotel in Lakewood, N.J., during Christmas recess. I looked up from the music and noticed a beautiful, tall young girl. I was smitten! I met her, we started to date and, as Julius Caesar said, "*Veni, Vidi, Vici*" I came, I saw, I conquered. At that time, I lived in the Bronx, and Gertrude lived in Newark, N.J., so every weekend, I made the long trip from the Bronx to Newark to be with my love. We were married eighteen months after we met.

After my graduation from college, it was decision time. The logical options available were either a career in music or, since I had a degree in business, becoming an accountant. In music, it was the era of the "big bands." I could join a band and travel the country. This would be a vagrant life. Furthermore, while I was a competent musician, I had no outstanding musical talent. All my forbearers had been business people. I loved the unlimited challenges and creativity of commercial enterprise. Accordingly, I retired my beloved saxophone. When I was drafted in 1942 during World War II, while I was stationed at Fort Dix for a period of three months, I took the sax out of retirement and played in the big Jack Leonard band. After that, the sax was relegated to closet after closet through the next twelve years as I went through my army and subsequent business career.

In 1955, I built a home for my family in Coral Gables, Florida. I was in the building and development business, so I built a nice 2,500 square foot house for a total cost of $7,500.00. Notice what the ravage of inflation hath wrought! The same house today would cost about $350,000.00. My saxophone reposed in our house closet until my wife presented me with an ultimatum. She needed that closet space or else dire consequences would ensue! I placed the sax in the trunk of my car. After a year, practicality trumped sentiment and the sax had to go. An acquaintance owned a large music store in Coral Gables so I went to his emporium, took my $7.00 Conn Sax, and lovingly placed it on the counter. "John" I said, "I want to sell this fine sax. I am not playing any longer. How much can you give me?" He looked at the instrument and told me that he would not buy it. Even though it was a fine sax and probably as good or better than a new horn, he couldn't sell it to his customers.

I told him the story of how this sax had put me through college and had been my companion for many years. I said, "John, I do not want any money. This instrument has sentimental value to me. I want you to promise that you will give this horn to the first poor kid that comes in and cannot afford to buy a sax." John burst out into uproarious laughter. He said "Jack, you are living in a world of the past. My store is in an area of affluent people. A kid comes in here, tugging his mother. He looks at my large display of shiny new instruments and he picks the most expensive one. The price tag is $1,200.00. He tells his mother that he wants that horn, and she whips out her checkbook and writes me a check for the full amount. However, Jack, since you have been honest with me, I will follow your wishes and I promise that I will find a poor kid and give him your horn." As I left the store I was happy that my sax would find a good adoptive home.

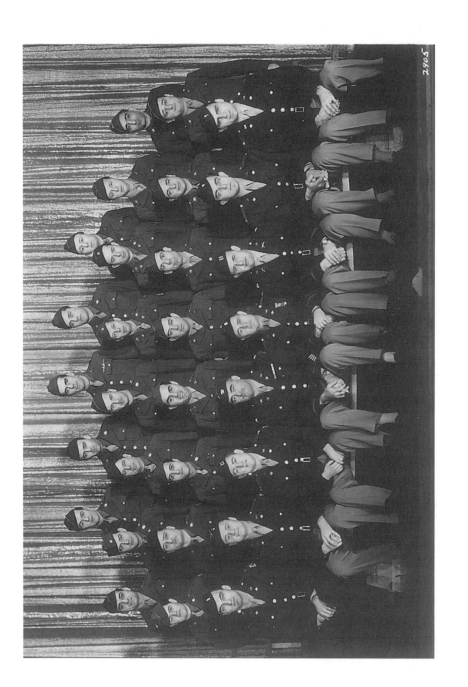

The author (upper right hand corner, last row) attending Army Finance College in 1944.

CHAPTER THREE

EDUCATION AND THE MILITARY

I graduated from college in 1940 with a B.B.A. degree in accounting. I searched for employment and finally obtained a job with a small C.P.A. firm. My salary was $10.00 per week. For this sum, I worked six and a half days a week. I went out on audits Monday through Friday. On Saturday I typed all the accounting reports. If I could not complete the reports on Saturday, occasionately I would have to come in Sunday to finish the jobs. My goal, of course, was to become a C.P.A. and eventually open my own practice. However, to become a C.P.A. three years experience working for a C.P.A. firm was required, in addition to passing a three-day C.P.A. exam. Therefore, employment by a C.P.A. firm was mandatory. The employee had no bargaining power. The employer paid sub-minimum wages to the professional college graduate. In addition to my day job, I also attended St. John's University, Brooklyn Law School, in the evenings. I was starting my law education, intending to become an attorney. When I graduated from college, because of good grades and interest in law, I had received a free, three-year scholarship to law school. I was on the go full time—working as an accountant every day in New York, going to law school at night in Brooklyn, and on weekends visiting with my girlfriend in Newark.

Enormous changes were on the horizon. World War II had started in Europe. On December 7, 1941, the Japanese attacked Pearl Harbor and the U.S. declared war on Japan and Germany. The U.S.A. was totally unprepared for this holocaust, and had a small inefficient army and navy. Because of the depression, spending for the military had been almost non-existent. Soldiers trained with wooden simulated rifles. The Army had a cavalry, still based on horses, and was just beginning to convert to small tanks. Suddenly the country required a fast and thorough build-up in men and war materials. To this end, Congress enacted a draft of all citizens. All males eighteen years and older were summoned to be physically examined and classified for call-up to military duty. I had married in July 1941, so I was not called immediately. However, I was summoned in December 1942. I reported to Camp Dix in New Jersey. Of course, my accounting career was terminated, and I had to quit law school. I was "in the army now." My military career began.

This required career change was awesome and challenging. It was very harmful in a personal sense because it terminated both my accounting career and my law school education. I had to spend the next four years in the service of Uncle Sam. The time when I left for camp was tearful for my new wife and fearful for me. It was quite obvious that our enemies played with real guns and every life was at stake! This was not the game we had played as kids on the streets of New York. I reported to Camp Dix in December, 1942. The thermometer recorded a freezing zero degrees. Because the war had just started, there were no barracks. We lived in tents, eight cots to a tent. The little space heater in the center of the tent could not keep us warm. Invariably, we would awaken at night with frostbitten toes or ears and run to sleep in the latrine building, which was well heated.

A professional person who evidently had some psychiatric training interviewed each inductee. It was his job to send each soldier to what he considered the most appropriate service and position, i.e., army, navy, infantry, engineers, etc. The interviewer looked at my educational background and assigned me to a special duty. I know it had to be a special job, for the following reason: Camp Dix was a reception center. The services were in dire need of soldiers and they needed them in a hurry. Each inductee who came to Ft. Dix was classified and, in three days, he was sent to his new assignment for training somewhere in the country. Therefore, when I found myself remaining at Dix for two and one-half months, I presume that they either lost my card or that, like a square peg in a round hole, I didn't fit any of their patterns.

The military was a fantastic experience! The broadening of lifetime experiences—traveling to different parts of the country, meeting diverse people, learning to live and work together with various individuals, amply compensated for the sacrifice of money and the termination of my career. This was experience that I could get only under military conditions where there was no choice but to follow the procedure and associate with people not of my choosing. It was a great leveler. Faced with this situation, all the survival skills learned in the "University of the Ghetto" came to the fore. As I smartly saluted my officer and said, "Yes Sir," I was secretly trying to figure out how to work my way out of the odious situations the officer was requiring of me. After three months of hanging around Camp Dix, sneaking off to the recreation center every morning, hiding every day so as not to work in the kitchen, my number finally came up. Along with a large contingent of other men, I was loaded onto a railroad cattle car. We tried to find out our destination, but no one would tell us. It was a military secret. After three days, we arrived at Camp Stewart, Georgia, where I was assigned to an anti-aircraft battery. Awakened at 5 A.M. after a good breakfast at the mess hall, we all hurried to the shooting range. We fed large shells into the anti-aircraft guns, trying to hit a target being towed by a small plane. This was hard, physically exhausting work. I had no intention of remaining a gun jockey! I called on my survival skills, and after a few days, I figured out a strategy. Our commanding officer was a Captain. As a private, I was not allowed to approach him. I needed permission from the First Sergeant. Fortunately, the First Sergeant was a copious beer drinker. After I bought him six beers, I got his permission to approach the Captain. The next morning I appeared before the Captain, saluted smartly, and made my pitch.

"Captain" I said, "I have been reading the military manual which clearly states that you, the commanding officer of this company, are responsible and personally liable for all property of the company. I also find that the men here are discarding or destroying materials which you may be personally charged for."

The Captain replied, "I know I am personally responsible, but I have no control over the material. I don't even know how much material we have in this company or where it is."

I continued "Captain, Sir, in civilian life I am a C.P.A., and I can help you take control and give you a complete daily report on all company material. Furthermore, I will set up a perpetual inventory system so that when your superiors ask you about the quantity of all materials, including bullets, guns, etc., you will have the information in front of you, on your desk, every morning." The Captain was pleased, bought my pitch, and the very next day, I was the supply sergeant. I had my own office in the company warehouse and a staff of several soldiers to dispense the materials needed by the troops. I faithfully set up an inventory system, and the Captain enjoyed my daily reports as much as I enjoyed trading sheets and pillowcases with the cooks in the kitchen for steak dinners. How could I have learned that at Harvard or Yale?

Success breeds more success! After several months as supply sergeant, I was anxious to move on. However, in the military service, there is a standard chain of command. You are not permitted to go over the head of your superior officer. If you do, you are liable for punishment or court martial. My immediate goal was to get transferred to the Finance Department at Camp Stewart. They had a large building and about fifty soldiers who prepared payrolls for the entire camp. All monthly payrolls to the soldiers were paid in cash. A great deal of mathematical work was necessary to compute each soldier's payroll. The commanding officer, Captain Walter Henderson, was one of the finest gentlemen I ever met. I decided to approach Captain Henderson without permission from my own officer. I was so bored with the stupid job I had created for myself that I figured the brig might be more stimulating than continuing my job. With much trepidation, I went to Captain Henderson's office, told him I could compute payrolls faster that any of his men, that I was a C.P.A. in private life and that all my life, education and experience were in finance. At that point, the captain had several choices. If he were a nice person, he could say "no" and tell me to leave. On the other hand, he could report me to my own captain for the proper military punishment. Or he could go out on a limb and request my transfer from the artillery unit to the Finance Department. Fortunately for me, he requested my transfer to the Finance Department, and I joyfully packed my belongings. I am sure that Captain Henderson paid a military price for having me transferred. I know that my former Captain raised the issue with headquarters. However, in the end, Captain Henderson prevailed and I was now a part of the Finance Department.

It became clear that if I wanted to survive in this military milieu, I had to "work the system." Even if I was not always successful, I had to try. Remember, a soldier has no positive control of his situation or status. Of course, I realized that we were at war and that it was necessary to do everything to win the conflict. So I worked diligently at all the positions to which I was assigned. At work in the Finance Office, I clearly was more competent than the other soldiers. By the time they figured one payroll, I had computed three. Captain Henderson noticed my work and gave me a promotion. Furthermore, he arranged an appointment for me to attend the Army Finance School at Fort Benjamin Harrison in Indianapolis. I spent two weeks there over Christmas and New Years, 1943. He further arranged my attendance at the Army Finance College at Wake Forest College in North Carolina. So in the first quarter of 1944, for three months, I attended school at Wake Forest College.

When I was assigned to the Finance Department, my wife Gertrude came down to Georgia to live with me. She got a job at Camp Stewart headquarters. Considering wartime conditions, we were living well. I worked at Finance, she worked at

Headquarters, and after work every day, we spent the evening together. I did not work weekends. I even purchased my first car, a used 1935 Ford. It cost only $75.00, but I spent many times that sum trying to get it to run.

I admit that I am a dedicated workaholic. I must keep busy day and night. As a young man, I required only six hours of sleep each night. Camp Stewart was about twenty-five miles from the delightful city of Savannah, Georgia. I was anxious to maintain my accounting career. Through the phone book, I located a C.P.A. firm in Savannah and was interviewed by a fine Southern gentleman who had a substantial C.P.A. practice. Most of his employees had been drafted and he was in dire need of help. He was happy that I was available on weekends, and he turned over a large amount of work to me. I enjoyed the accounting jobs and I was happy. My boss was a wonderful gentleman. He did not give me a salary. Instead, he gave me the entire fee on every job that I completed, and he never withheld a dime. He even assigned a bank audit job to me, for which I received the full fee. We had a nice arrangement. However, when the Army sent me to Wake Forest College in early 1944, I reluctantly bid my boss good-bye. I sold my car, and my wife and I moved to Wake Forest, North Carolina.

Wake Forest College was totally taken over by the military during the war. It was the Army Finance War College and provided a three-month course in Army Finance. Several hundred soldiers were stationed there. The work was rigorous, but I loved being back at school. I am a life-long student. Stationed there, my wife made many friends with the wives of the other soldiers. A martinet colonel commanded the wartime college. I was back in the army. Every day at 4 P.M., after school, we stood "full retreat." With the army band playing, in full uniform, we paraded across the drill field, saluted and raised the flag amid much pomp and ceremony. After three months, I returned to my job at the Finance Office at Camp Stewart. Unfortunately, Captain Henderson was no longer there. It was spring of 1944. The war was hot. The allies were preparing for the invasion of Europe. Captain

Henderson, always the fine patriotic gentleman, had requested field duty and had been sent overseas.

With the impending invasion of Europe, the military needed every soldier overseas. An order came through from Supreme Command that all soldiers in the U.S.A. who were 1A (meaning the soldier was in good physical condition) were to be trained and sent overseas. I was 1A, and I was ordered to pack my bags. I was being transferred to the 82nd Airborne Parachute battalion. I was twenty-four years old and I had never done any physical work in my life. I couldn't picture myself parachuting out of an airplane. With great trepidation, I prepared for the worst. There was no more maneuvering. I had come up against a solid wall. I packed all my gear. As I was preparing to leave, I received a phone call from a soldier friend of mine who worked at headquarters. He told me that they had just received urgent orders to hold all C.P.A.s in this country and refrain from sending them overseas. The government had run into a problem. The entire country was producing vast quantities of war materials, guns, ammunition, planes, vehicles, tanks, ships, etc. Each item produced was governed by a contract between the government and the industrialist. Very often changes were necessary in the production process because of experiences in the field. For example, suppose a factory was producing shells for guns. In the field these shells were exploding prematurely or were malfunctioning. The contract was cancelled, and a new contract was issued for a newer version of the shell. The contractor filed a claim for compensation due for the expenses and costs that he had expended to produce the cancelled contract. Someone had to audit the contractor's claim and approve payment. The military needed auditors for this function. Accordingly, they put out a call for all C.P.A.s in the military to be held in this country to audit these cancelled government contracts.

Instead of becoming a parachutist with the Eighty-Second Airborne, I was sent to Pittsburgh as an auditor for the Pittsburgh Ordinance District. There were over three thousand employees in the District. They were engaged in ordering all sorts of military supplies. Since Pittsburgh at that time was the steel and manufacturing center of the country, thousands of military contracts were being issued every week, and hundreds of contracts a month were being terminated. I was assigned to audit contracts that had been terminated to verify reimbursement to the contractors. The head of the accounting division at the Pittsburgh Ordinance District was William Muchow. As the former senior partner of the accounting firm, Peat, Marwick, Mitchell, etc., Mr. Muchow had been selected to head up the military accounting department at the district. There were approximately two hundred accountants under his command. Because of my accounting and legal background, I was one of the most qualified auditors in the office. On several of the cases assigned to me, I discovered fraudulent claims and brought this to the attention of my superiors. As a result, Bill Muchow came to respect my accounting abilities, and he assigned to me the larger and more difficult audits. For example, I was sent to audit the books of U.S. Steel Corporation, at that time the largest steel company in the world. They refused to permit me examine their books. I persisted. However, they had enough political clout to prevent their books from being opened to scrutiny. I was ordered by my superiors to accept the figures they submitted.

The government had drafted all industry. The government had a program known as "Renegotiation" by which all companies performing government work had their financial statements audited every year. The financial statements were reviewed, and the auditor determined a suggested "refund" to the government. For example, the government "re-negotiator" would usually allow a profit of 7% to 9%, depending on the performance of the company. The "re-negotiator" accountant had to scrutinize and thoroughly audit the financial statements submitted by the company to determine the accuracy of the statements. When a position became available in the "renegotiation" department, Bill Muchow appointed me to this position. It was an awesome responsibility. There were only seven men in this department, all civilian employees. As a civilian, the civil service category for this job was CAF 13, the highest government pay category. However, as a soldier, I was only a sergeant, earning a measly seventy-five dollars a month. Having been assigned audits of seven of the largest companies in the country, such as U.S. Steel, Allegheny Ludlum, etc., I did, however have the use of a government car for travel to various industrial facilities. Since my specialty at college had been cost accounting, I really enjoyed the work, and because of my experience, I was able to complete the audits thoroughly and timely, which left me plenty of time for personal matters.

When I was renegotiating a very large company, Allegheny Ludlum, I discussed my findings with the president of the company. I informed him that I was recommending that the company refund two hundred million dollars to the government. Noticing that I was in uniform as a sergeant, he asked why the government had sent a sergeant to audit his company and recommend such a large refund. I answered that while I was a sergeant in the army, I was a C.P.A. in civilian life, and of course, I had no control over my rank in the service. He picked up the phone and called the commanding officer of the large Pittsburgh Ordinance District. He said "Colonel Downey, how come the army sends a sergeant to my company who is requesting this huge sum of money? Isn't the government ashamed to assign this task to a sergeant?" Colonel Downey got the message, and two weeks later I was appointed a Warrant Officer in the army. Immediately on becoming an officer, my pay and privileges were greatly enhanced

When the army sent me to Pittsburgh, my wife Gertrude had come along to live with me. She took a job with the district and we were living rather well, considering wartime conditions. Happily, in December 1945, we were blessed with the birth of our first son, Mark, born in Allegheny General Hospital in Pittsburgh. At the time, we were living in an apartment in McKees Rocks in a low-cost government housing project. For the next nine months, I spent all my free time helping to care for our son.

In 1945, the U.S. dropped the atom bomb on Japan. The war was won, hostilities ceased, and soldiers were released back to civilian life. Because of my job, I had to remain to clean up many ongoing projects and audits. Therefore, I was not released until October 1946. My army boss, Bill Muchow, had returned to head the C.P.A. firm of Peat, Marwick, Mitchell, etc. He offered me a job with a substantial salary and the promise of becoming a partner in the future. I declined. I wanted to return to New Jersey to be with my wife and family. When I was finally released from the service in October 1946, we loaded our old 1937 Pontiac with our meager belongings, and our family of three headed back home to New Jersey to an unknown but challenging future.

CHAPTER FOUR

OPERATING AN ACCOUNTING PRACTICE

It was October 1946. My wife Gertrude, my son, Mark, and I arrived back in our pre-war town of Newark, N.J. Buying or renting an apartment or a house was impossible. During the war, all building construction had ceased, and housing units were unobtainable. We moved into my father-in-law's house where we had one room for the three of us. It was tight, but we were together. I was happy to be free of the army discipline, and for the first time in four years, I felt that we were in control of our own destiny. However, our life's savings were only $1,000. I needed to get some steady income soon.

At that point our future did not look very promising. Financially we were almost broke. During my four years in the army we had lived on subsistence earnings. Now, it was imperative that I plan ahead for the future and get some immediate income. I was tired of working for other people. I was offered a job by the accounting firm that I had left when I was drafted, but the pay was pitiful. I felt that it was time to get started on a solid future. Since we had no money, I knew that it would be an uphill battle, but I was determined. I wanted to return to law school to complete my education, but financially that was out of the question. I had a family to support.

I decided to start my own accounting business. My brother Jules who had left the accounting firm for which he worked, was also anxious to start a new enterprise. So we decided to work together and in our own accounting firm.

We both went to work full time. Jules had a few clients for a start, but we had to aggressively search for new accounts. We had many schemes to obtain clients. For example, we researched the public records for new businesses, and we contacted them by mail and by personal visits; we ran down every possible lead; we asked everyone for recommendations; we printed up fliers to distribute to prospective clients. Over the next few years, we built a substantial clientele and had a successful accounting business. After several more years, our practice had grown to the point where we hired several accountant employees. Jules and I were a great team since we both had the same perspective and goals. We were going to build a successful business. I determined to work round the clock, if necessary. All the frustrations of working as an employee, being told how to do a job, and how to think were now in the past.

From a business standpoint we had a problem. Jules was married to Edythe, a charming lady whom Jules had married during the war. Edythe was a very successful business lady who had managed a large factory in New York City and earned a substantial salary, much more than her husband earned at his accounting business. After marriage, Edythe had left her job and settled down as a housewife. For a long time, she was unhappy with being a homebody. With her business talent, she missed managing an enterprise, and so she was continually trying to get Jules to go into other businesses in addition to our accounting practice. In fact, when we started our accounting business, Jules and Edythe were partners in a retail liquor store in Long Island. The geographical area of our accounting business quickly spread from northern New Jersey, through New York City and into Long Island. I lived in Union, New Jersey, and I serviced all the accounts in New Jersey. I also drove to New York and Long Island several times a week to help Jules service our accounts in that area. Originally I had no objection to this arrangement. Anything I could do to help my brother was all right with me. I was a workaholic anyway.

We built our practice until we had several hundred clients and were starting to progress financially. Jules sold his liquor store partnership and all was well. However, one of our clients was Frank Nocella, a tough, little fellow who owned a restaurant just opposite the Belmont Race Track. Frank was a personable man. However, he was always surrounded by a coterie of tough mob-looking individuals. I steered clear of those fellows. One guy was so powerful that when a huge bank-type vault had to be moved, he single-handedly completed the job. Anyway, Frank talked Jules into going, as partners, into a nightclub business in the adjoining city of Franklin Square. The club was named "El Mambo." Edythe was thrilled, since at last, she could work and operate the business. Jules and Edythe spent afternoons, evenings and nights at the club. As a result I spent more and more of my time taking over the accounting tasks that Jules was supposed to perform. After a while I was doing the work of two people, working round the clock, traveling from my home in New Jersey to handle not only my clients, but also Jules's clients. It was not fair to me and, from a physical standpoint, I couldn't continue at this pace for long.

It became apparent after a while that being involved in the nightclub business was beyond the capabilities of Jules and Edythe. It was a full time job, day and night and they had family obligations. Some of the characters who were customers and hung out at the bar were mafia members with such names like two-finger Louie, etc. Many times, when Jules tended bar, these customers would offer, "Jules, if you want someone's arm broken, or someone messed up, we'll do it as a favor for you since you are a regular fellow." The club was also a money loser. So eventually Jules and Edythe ended their exotic career as nightclub impresarios. At that time, I had a heart-to-heart discussion with Jules. I told him that I never had nor would I ever have outside business interests; that I was gung-ho on building a successful business; that going into other enterprises would just detract and jeopardize our entire business future. We were partners and we should have no outside business interests. We could make more money by concentrating on our own business. We agreed. So, in the early fifties, we both decided to sell our accounting practices and start a new life in Florida.

From 1946 through 1953 our accounting business in New York and New Jersey had flourished. We had several hundred clients. Most needed to be serviced every month. During this entire period, I worked from early morning until late into the evening. During income tax season, from December 1st to March 15th, I toiled all day and into the early mornings—2 or 3 A.M., seven days a week. Although we had a nice house in Union, New Jersey, I was getting tired of the terrible northern weather. In winter it turned dark at 5 P.M., and usually we were confined indoors for the evening. When it snowed, the snow bank blocked the garage door and I couldn't get the car out of the garage. When I first saw Florida and spent a week on vacation in 1950, I determined to move our family.

In 1948, after living in one room for over a year, we finally found an all-brick two-story house, in Union, New Jersey, priced at $14,000.00. I hadn't enough money for the $1,000.00 down payment. However, my father-in-law advanced the money to close the deal. I have been back to see that house several times over the past fifty years. The house is still there, in pristine condition, but the price now is $300,000.00. Not only did we acquire a new home, but soon thereafter, we welcomed a new addition to our family when son Jeffrey was born.

After my service in the army I felt an obligation to become active in politics in the small town of Union, New Jersey where we lived. The Mayor was Hugo Biertumpel, a Republican, and a powerful political figure that completely controlled the town with an iron hand. At that time I wanted to become active in the local Democratic Party. I attended a meeting of the local Democrats and I discovered that there were only seven individuals in the party. I also discovered that Mayor Biertumpel had wisely bought them off. I decided that it was time to rebuild the Democratic Party in Union. I visited many of the neighbors and returned veterans, and in a few years, we built a strong local Democratic party. Since I was regarded as the leader, I attended many of the statewide Democratic conferences and became the Democratic leader of Union County. Biertumpel was still too powerful to defeat locally. I ran for School Board and after receiving threatening phone calls aimed at my small children and also myself, I realized that politics was a dirty business. I was defeated for School Board. However, our Democratic party was very successful in 1952 when we elected the first Democratic governor of New Jersey in one hundred years, Robert Meyner. I was offered the position of Democratic Leader of Union County. This was an important job, but I was already planning to go to Florida. I recommended a friend who had worked hard for the party for that position.

Jules and I had built up a fairly large accounting practice. I believe that if one is a good teacher, the teacher also learns from the students. As a C.P.A., I would be the "teacher." I would review all the financial figures with my clients and guide them to make intelligent business decisions. In this regard I will now tell you the story of two of my most successful clients because I learned a great deal about business from them.

Emile Mouhot was the owner of a very large electrical contracting company called North Shore Electric Company situated in the Hempstead area of Long Island. North Shore Electric was the foremost electrical contractor on the island and every year the company wired several thousand houses, industrial plants, schools, etc. After the war, there was a huge building boom all over the country, especially in New York. The city was expanding out on Long Island. Levitt and Sons were the largest homebuilder in the country, building over 6,000 homes each year. The houses sold for $6,200.00 each. Emile's company was the electrical contractor for all of Levitt's homes. Levitt wanted all his contractors to produce innovative ideas to reduce his costs. Emile always came up with new electric fixtures, a redesign of the electrical pattern or some other innovation that permitted Levitt to save money. In addition to his Levittown work, Emile also worked for most of the other large builders on Long Island, and that presented a problem. Most of the builders required union electricians. Levitt was a non-union builder. Emile solved his problem by setting up a non-union company called W.A.Anderson

Co. that did all of Levitt's work. North Shore Electric was union and was able to build for all the other union builders on the island.

Emile had entered his father's business at the age of sixteen. He never had finished high school. He learned the electrical contracting business very rapidly, and when Levitt started his large-scale housing development known as Levittown, Emile came in with the lowest bid and won the contract. Levitt never changed to other electrical contractors because Emile's company was always on schedule and innovative, both in improving the product and in saving Levitt money.

Now let me tell you about this man's business genius. Having a licensed union electrician go to the site, assemble all the material and supplies, and put the system together was the usual electrical installation. Emile realized how inefficient and costly this plan was, so he changed the system. He set up an in-house operation and a field operation. He hired minimum-wage individuals in-house to sit at long tables, cutting and installing the wires and tubing to each socket. Each wire and tube was cut to the proper size. The factory workers then attached the metal boxes containing the sockets. Emile sent his trucks to the construction site, each truck manned by two "slingers." The "slingers" were non-skilled laborers who were taught just one job, to sling the rough wiring over the ceiling beams and throughout the house. Following behind them quickly were semi-skilled laborers who attached the pre-cut internal wires. Only then, in the final stage, did a "real" electrician, a highly paid master electrician, earning many times the wages of the factory worker, come to the job to attach the main electrical panel and the plastic plates on the boxes to complete the installation.

Emile made millions of dollars in profits from his business. His one blind spot was that he was so conservative that he believed only in cash in the bank. He refused to invest money in almost all ventures that were presented to him. I noticed that he always had a million dollars in his checking account. All invoices were paid in ten days—no waiting for the tenth of the month. The most brilliant thing I remember about Emile is that at a meeting he set up with me, he discussed a forward-looking idea he had developed. He wanted to discuss a new business plan that he had in mind. He asked me if I could set up the required cost-accounting system that was necessary to accomplish this new plan. I explained that cost accounting had been my real forte at college and I surely could set up a foolproof system. Emile said "Jack, we are losing a great amount of material that is discarded on the job. Furthermore my eight foremen are inefficient in using their assigned workers. We are wasting large amounts of money. I have come up with a new plan to solve these problems but I need you to set up eight different sets of books—one for each of my foremen. I will give each foreman his own large trailer truck. We will stock his van with materials that will be charged to him. We will also charge the labor he uses to his account and we will give him a share of the profits on each job if he exceeds the current rate of profit." This high-school dropout had devised an excellent plan for establishing the most efficient, most cost effective operation possible.

I thought his plan was exceptionally brilliant, and I agreed to set up the necessary accounting records. Emile called his eight foremen into the office. He said "Fellows, many of you have been with this company for a long time but I regret to tell you that you are all now fired." He continued, "That is the bad news. However, the good news is that you are all now in business for yourselves. You each will have your own trailer; you can order all the material you need from the warehouse; you can hire your own employees. It is up to you to run your business in the most efficient manner. Every three months, Mr. Freeman will audit the books of your operation and we will give you a generous percentage of the earnings you have achieved in running your operation." The foremen were thrilled. They watched every piece of material that they were charged with; no employee goofed off. Performance and profits zoomed. Every three months, the foremen were rewarded, but Emile's business was the greatest beneficiary!

There was an enormous amount of building in post-war Long Island. North Shore Electric was bidding on a dozen or more big jobs all the time, such as industrial factories, schools, and municipal projects. In almost every case, North Shore Electric was the high bidder. Yet each year Emile's North Shore Electric Co. managed to get a major portion of these jobs. I asked Emile "Your bid is so much higher than the low bid. How do you manage to get these jobs with such high profitability?" Emile replied, "Jack, I can get every one of these jobs, but they would be at break-even or loss and I don't want that. I would rather have none of those jobs. On the other hand, each municipality or commercial entity generally gives the job to the lowest "responsible" bidder. Each bidder must be able to provide a large performance bond to assure quality work and ability to complete the project. Performance bonds can run into multi-million dollars. In many cases my competitors are not financially able to provide that performance bond. As the lowest "responsible" bidder I usually get three or four of the dozen jobs I bid on and I manage to make more money on those jobs than if I were the successful low bidder on all of them."

As you can see, my admiration for Emile Mouhot was boundless! However, here is one more almost unbelievable but true story about Emile. He owned a ninety-foot yacht. Every October he headed his boat to Florida and tied up at Bahai Mar Marina in Fort Lauderdale. He remained in Florida on his yacht from October till April of every year. He ran his gigantic business by phone, from his yacht, for a six-month period. In his stead, he put his younger brother in charge of daily operations at the main office in Long Island.In all respects, Emile Mouhot was a business genius.

Another of our largest and most successful accounting clients was World Airways, the largest non-scheduled airline in the country. Edward Daly was the aggressive young man who put this airline together. His is the story of one man's determination to succeed in his dream to revolutionize the nascent aviation business. When World War II terminated, there were hundreds of thousands of air corps officers returning to civilian life. Many of them had become ace pilots and were determined to continue as pilots in civilian life. However, only two airlines existed in the United States and these were completely inadequate to handle the burgeoning demand for air travel. So ace pilots, returning to civilian status, besieged Congress with demands to expand the airline industry. Accordingly, Congress passed legislation to permit the formation of new airlines, to be known as "non-scheduled" airlines. Any pilot with a three-cent stamp and the proper paperwork could get a "Certificate of Necessity" issued by the government permitting the formation of a new airline. Seventy-three "Certificates" were issued before the entire transportation industry, the existing regular airlines, the railroads and bus companies vehemently attacked this new program. The government realized the enormity of the monster it had created. It cancelled the program and campaigned to withdraw the certificates that it had issued. Eventually the government succeeded in canceling almost all of the certificates. However, there still remained eight "non-scheduled" airline certificates in force.

Edward Daly had not been born into wealth and glory. This proud, smart and very tough Irish-American was born in Chicago in 1923 and bred in humble surroundings. After the war, Ed was employed in a New York travel agency, and he witnessed the enormous pent up demand for travel and the inability of the existing systems to fulfill that demand. Ed determined to obtain a "Certificate of Necessity" and go into the airline business, but he had no money. He put out feelers to find investors. Ed Daly approached one of our clients, Sam Keenholtz, as a possible investor. Sam, my brother Jules, and I decided to back Ed in this venture and we raised about $25,000.00. Ed left his job, went to Florida and was able to obtain a certificate in the name of World Airways. However, Ed was unable to obtain any aircraft so he returned dejectedly to New York. Since he had left his job and had spent most of the remaining funds on expenses, we, the investors, turned over the certificate to him and wrote off the balance of the investment as a loss.

However, Ed was a determined, bright, aggressive young man. Over the next several months he was able to negotiate a lease for two C-46 airplanes from the government and he started his airline. Shortly after the termination of World War II, the government had thousands of airplanes that were returned to this country and were either "mothballed" or stationed at remote airfields in Texas and out west. The C-46 planes were large twin-engine transportation workhorses that had carried troops and cargo all over the world. Each airplane had cost the government millions of dollars and most were still in excellent condition. The end of the war had made them expendable. The government decided to lease each plane for the paltry sum of $150.00 per month. Among the first group to take advantage of this offer was a non-scheduled airline called the "Flying Tigers" of World War II fame. The Tigers used the planes to haul cargo. Ed Daly and World Airways leased two C-46 planes from the government at $150.00 per month per plane. He upgraded the interior of each plane, installing 53 removable passenger seats so that he could use the planes to transport passengers. If he had to fly cargo, he removed the seats and converted to a cargo configuration. World Airways at that time flew little cargo. It was the late forties and early fifties and hundreds of thousands of Puerto Ricans were leaving their tropical island and coming to New York. I would venture to guess that World Airways, in that time period, was largely responsible for populating New York City with Puerto Ricans.

I had lost track of Ed Daly until I received a call from him in October 1950. He wanted to see me at LaGuardia Airport where he was operating his two planes. He wanted me to become the accountant for the airline because his records were in a mess. He was so busy flying his two planes to Puerto Rico up and back that he had no time to keep proper books. I went to work for him and set up a proper accounting system. The company was making money, but the expenses and costs to upgrade and maintain the planes were eating up all the cash. At that time there was a 10% U.S. tax on all passenger transportation. In auditing the records, I discovered that World Airways had not paid any of this tax and owed the government over $ 300,000.00. This was an enormous sum and the money to pay this tax was certainly not available. I told Ed that the proper thing to do was to file the delinquent reports, acknowledge the debt and make arrangements to pay the government the taxes due, over a period of time. I believed that if the IRS was notified of the taxes due and the financial situation of the business, a payment schedule could be arranged that would be compatible with the cash flow.

When I approached Ed and told him that we should file the delinquent forms and acknowledge the debt to the IRS, I thought Ed and I were going to part company. If Ed did not permit me to file the tax forms with the IRS, I informed him that I could not continue as his accountant. Reluctantly he accepted my plan. I personally did not feel good about this situation. If the IRS refused to go along with my plan, I would have, in effect, bankrupted the newly born airline. However, Ed personally would be in legal trouble if he failed to file the required tax returns. I am sure that Ed did not appreciate my intervention at that time but he decided to go along with the plan. Years later when World Airways was a huge, and prosperous airline, Ed finally thanked me for filing the tax forms and getting him straight with the government. If he had not settled at that time, the airline would have been out of business. I was able to work with the IRS even though it took many trips to the Brooklyn office of the IRS, but we finally paid off the delinquent taxes.

I was the accountant and financial advisor to Ed Daly and World Airways from its inception in 1949 until I left for Florida in 1954. As the airline grew, I spent many days and evenings at World Airways. There were constant problems with the government. The Civil Air Board (CAB) was in complete control of the airline industry. At the urging of the scheduled airlines, the railroads and the trucking industry, they maintained a constant campaign to put the few "non-scheduled" airlines out of business. I spent many days and evenings preparing the copious government reports necessary to keep the company in business.

On occasion, Ed, my brother Jules, and I would go to
Washington to appear before the CAB. Ed was a fun-loving
individual. He and I became fast friends. Ed said he did not care
to be a millionaire; he just wanted to live like one. He achieved
both dreams. In fact, he became a very successful multi-millionaire.
I recall that on one trip to Washington, his office made reservations
for us at a hotel. Ed booked the presidential suite that had a
grand piano in the living room. As a poor kid from the Bronx,
being in a hotel room with a grand piano was well beyond my
wildest dreams! In many respects, Ed was annoying to work with.
He was a "night person." He slept all day and worked all evening
and throughout the night, meeting his business contacts in
nightclubs in New York and making his deals in that environment.
Invariably, when I was working at the World Airway office at
Teterboro Airport, I would get a call from Ed at about 5 P.M. just
as I was ready to go home, Ed, who had just awakened, would
say "Jack, let's go out and get a bowl of soup." Ed had been out
all night drinking with his business contacts at the best New
York nightclubs, making deals, buying and selling airplanes, etc.
I reluctantly went out for the "bowl of soup" at 5 P.M. and we
discussed all the financial problems of the airline over dinner.

After I left for Florida, Ed called me many times and offered
me all kinds of money, stock ownership, etc. to return to New
Jersey and be his accountant again. However, I was very happy
with my new development business in Florida and I would never
think of returning north. Under Ed's tutelage World Airways
was to become the largest charter airline in the world. When the
Vietnam War started, the government sent hundreds of thousands
of soldiers to that theatre. To transport the troops, the government
started a "MATS" program. Every day at the Pentagon, the army
would post a list of flights that were required to send and return
troops from Vietnam. World Airways obtained most of the
contracts, even though Daly was bidding against Pan Am, Eastern
Airlines and all the other major carriers. Ed was smart enough to
hire retired Air Force Generals to work for him and bid on these
military flight programs. World Airways became one of the largest

airlines in the world. Ed moved his operations from Teterboro Airport in New Jersey to Oakland California and built a huge headquarters and maintenance facility there. He also had overseas headquarters at Gatwick Airport outside of London. World Airways eventually employed thousands of pilots, stewardesses, and other airline employees.

I have related the stories of only two of my largest clients. Our accounting firm had several hundred clients. Each business presented unique problems that we learned to handle and solve. However, Jules and I felt that it was time to move on. We both wanted to live in Florida. For all our work and effort in the accounting field, we felt that we were just the "hired help" and that we would never be well enough compensated for our efforts. Therefore, we set up a plan to sell our accounting practice and head for the sunny South!

MY MOTTO :

"People who say

It cannot be done

Should not

Interrupt those who

Are doing it."

CHAPTER FIVE

STARTING A NEW CAREER IN FLORIDA

In October 1954 I finally arrived in Florida. I had first visited Miami in March 1950. I was living in New Jersey, working as a CPA, with my brother Jules, in our accounting practice in New York and New Jersey.

But I hated living in the congested New York-New Jersey area. I spent hours traveling through the Lincoln and Holland tunnels, bumper-to-bumper city driving; battling the snow in winter; staying at home evenings because darkness came at 5 PM in winter. After four years in the army, from 1942 to 1946, I had returned home from Pittsburgh where I had been stationed and spent the next four years building an accounting practice in New Jersey, New York and Long Island. I had no time for vacations. Finally in March 1950, I took my wife and two sons on a ten-day vacation to Miami, Florida.

Miami in 1950 seemed like paradise. The weather was beautiful and the southern laid-back atmosphere contrasted sharply with hurly-burly New York. We spent many hours on the beach and some time fishing in the wonderful sun-drenched city. I immediately decided that I would return north, sell my accounting practice and move to Florida. My brother Jules readily agreed. Therefore, we put our accounting practice up for sale and quickly sold it. However, as part of the deal, I had to introduce the buyer to our clients, and stay with him for a year until the new buyer was firmly in control of the business.

Jules and I had a plan. I would stay with the business until October 1954. Jules would move to Miami in 1953 and survey the opportunities for new ventures in Florida. Accordingly, in 1953, I traveled to Florida several times, and Jules and I traveled together throughout the southern portion of the state from Orlando south, looking for land. Our objective was to research various business opportunities in Florida, mainly in the real estate area, such as building or land development.

We traveled through all of South Florida looking for real estate opportunities. Just as we were researching these opportunities, fortunately for us, The *Miami Herald* solved all our problems and put us in business! Today, as I read the daily papers, I am struck with the apparent ignorance of most journalists. These "muckrakers" love controversial stories even though the truth may differ completely from what they print. In 1953, the *Miami Herald* had their star reporter do a series on the "crooked" real estate promoters who were selling so-called "swamp land" to northern buyers. Day after day, their reporter, Steven Trumbull, detailed how these greedy developers were bilking the public by selling worthless, swampland lots for $500.00, $10.00 dollars down and $10.00 a month. Today in year 2003, all these lots are improved with homes, commercial buildings, stores, etc. Today, if anyone could find an undeveloped lot in the same areas, the price would be at least $30,000 or more for the lot that sold for $500.

Steven Trumbull and the *Miami Herald* had, in particular, chosen to highlight as dishonest projects and developers, M.H. Davis of Naples Park and another developer in Venice, a city south of Sarasota. Jules and I were interested in seeing these "dishonest" developers, so we went to Naples and Venice. In our opinion, the developers were selling properties at "give-a-way" prices. If the money had been available, I would personally have bought all their lots. So the *Miami Herald* and Steven Trumbull put us in business. Then and there, we decided that we were going to purchase property in Florida and become developers.

Our next step was to find land for a viable development project. Our funds were limited. All we had was ten thousand dollars, so we had to pick land that had a special attraction for northern buyers. They were the predominant customers. We traveled the state. First, we went to Orlando, at that time, devoid of people. There were just two buildings in what is now downtown Orlando. As we drove the forty miles to Daytona Beach, all we saw were cows. It was real cowboy, cattle country. We were offered 10,000 acres on the Indian River, including what is now Cape Canaveral, for $10.00 per acre. Since it seemed unlikely that we could at that time sell this land, we turned down the offer. In retrospect, I sometimes dream of what would have happened if we owned Merritt Island and Cape Canaveral and could charge the government rent for every space vehicle lift-off!

After looking at properties all over South Florida, we finally selected the Ft. Myers area as having the most promising development potential. At that time W.Reynolds Real Estate was the largest broker in the area, so we asked Bill Reynolds to find us the property we needed. With only a few thousand dollars to spend, there was a limit to the amount of property we could purchase. In 1953, land on the southwest coast of Florida was selling for around $10.00 per acre for farmland. Almost all the land was in cattle ranches, usually in parcels of at least 1,000 acres or more.

Having decided to develop our project in Ft. Myers, we researched the area. One man, W. R. Frizell, owned most of the land in a three-county area—Lee, Charlotte and DeSoto counties. As I drove through Ft. Myers, I noticed Frizell owned most of the businesses: the farm equipment company, the Ford agency, etc. Mr. Frizell owned, along with other properties, 70,000 acres in Charlotte County stretching from Route #41(the Tamiami Trail) over to Boca Grande; 21,000 acres on Route #31, just south of Arcadia; and 10,000 acres in eastern Lee County. Because Frizell had some personal family situations that had to be resolved to protect his estate, he had put all these properties up for sale in the years 1952-1953.

Frizell sold the 21,000 acres on Route #31 to Nat Wolf, a citrus grower in Lakeland, Florida. The going price was $8.00 per acre or $168,000. Louis Chesler had purchased the 70,000 acres in Charlotte County for around $10.00 per acre. It was a beautiful property with miles of waterfront on the Peace River. Chesler immediately resold this property for $20.00 per acre to the Mackle Brothers, who at that time were large and respected real estate developers in Florida. They started General Development Corp. and developed this land into what is today the thriving city known as Port Charlotte.

The 10,000 acres in eastern Lee County was sold to Lee Ratner, a successful entrepreneur and businessman who had made most of his fortune by developing and selling "D-Con," a pesticide that killed rats. Every farmer in the country had purchased D-Con during and after WWII because it utilized a medicinal discovery of WWII that thinned the blood. By incorporating this medicine into a pesticide, the rats died as their blood "thinned out." Lee Ratner was an accomplished marketing man, and he took the 10,000 acres for which he had paid $10 per acre and developed it into "Lehigh Acres." The amazing thing in my mind is that today, Lehigh Acres has as many as 45,000 people; Lee Ratner developed and sold the entire project in the 1950s, and today, nobody even knows his name.

Bill Reynolds finally located a property that suited our meager pocket book and our development need. We purchased 240 acres for $40.00 an acre for a total price of $9,600, and paid the seller $3,000 down. The seller took a $6,600 mortgage, payable over ten years at 4% interest. The reason we paid $40.00 (a high price) was that the property was located on US#41, also known as the Tamiami Trail, the main road from Miami to Tampa. The approximately quarter mile of frontage on the "Trail" made the property much more valuable.

Remember that my brother and I were accountants. We knew nothing about marketing, building, or developing. Yet we owned the 240 acres. We had to learn not only how to sell, but also how to develop: plan the development, clear the land, build the road, drain the property with canals, etc. To accomplish the marketing, we arranged a meeting with Lee Ratner. He already had started his development, and he recommended that we consult his advertising agency. They could arrange the marketing program. Accordingly, we met with Irwin Harris who was president of Harris and Co., an advertising agency located on Lincoln Road in Miami Beach. Incidentally, at a later date, when Castro took over Cuba, he hired Harris and Company to do some good-will advertising for Cuba. Castro never paid Harris for the advertising. Irwin Harris was not about to let this two-bit dictator get away with it, so he impounded a Cuban airplane that was in Key West. In that fashion, he collected from Castro. However, since Castro had promised to "get him," Irwin carried a gun at all times.

Irwin introduced us to one of his top executives, Milt Mendelsohn. At the time, I did not know that Milt was a genius at marketing. In our initial marketing conference, we informed Milt that our total available budget was eight thousand dollars. He said that three thousand dollars would be required for the production of a brochure and that the balance of five thousand dollars would be used to advertise in Northern newspapers in the Sunday editions. At that time, almost all Florida properties were being sold to northern buyers. In the fifties, people had just been through four years of WWII warfare. Food, gasoline, tires, etc. had all been rationed. All automobile production had been halted from 1942 through year 1946 during the war. Now, with the war over, everyone was at work and all the shortages that had occurred during war suddenly needed to be filled. With the factories going at full blast, the workers now had disposable income, looking for opportunities to invest.

The most productive market for Florida land sales was in the northern industrial belt, Ohio, Michigan, and Indiana. Milt was going to advertise in the Sunday papers in these states. Of course, all the advertising was done during the winter months when the snow was on the ground and people were yearning for warm, sunny Florida. We had a meager five thousand dollars to spend, so we urged Milt to spread the advertising over a period of a few weeks.

We had planned our subdivision, and we named it "San Carlos Park." I had worked with the best engineer in Ft. Myers, Carl

Johnson. Carl had platted the land into approximately 800 lots. This is the property we had for sale. Meanwhile, I had set up a mailing address in Ft. Myers so that all our mail would be sent to that office. Our advertisement described our beautiful development, and gave the customer the privilege of purchasing a lot. In one fell swoop, for a deposit of $10, he became a landowner in Florida. We requested that the purchaser send the $10 down payment to our mailing address. The marketing psychology was awesome. For $10, the typical customer who worked in an auto plant in Ohio or Michigan could brag to his boss and his friends that he was a man of substance, because he owned "property in Florida."

So Milt Mendelsohn, our advertising man, was going to place the ads in December 1954 in newspapers in Ohio and Michigan. We insisted that the ads be placed over a period of four weeks on Sundays. However, Milt did not listen to our conservative program. Unbeknown to us, he placed all our five thousand dollars worth of ads in one Sunday. When I found out, I was outraged! What if there was a blizzard on that Sunday and people could not get their newspapers? What if there were events up north on that day, and people did not read their newspapers? All the "what ifs" actually materialized and we saw our five thousand dollars go down the drain. I was fighting mad. I went to Milt's office and unloaded on him all the choice language I had learned as a kid in the Bronx streets. However, the die was cast and visions of failure in my first Florida venture had apparently materialized!

The ads appeared on one Sunday in December. On Wednesday following, I went to my office in Ft. Myers, dejected by the thought that our five thousand dollars, in one fell swoop, was wasted. But in front of our office, were three completely full mailbags. When I lugged them into the office and opened the envelopes, coupons and ten-dollar checks were enclosed. Ten-dollar checks were lying all over the floor! In that one-day of advertising, we had sold all 800 lots. I then realized Milt was a real marketing genius. I went to Milt's office and apologized.

Milt Mendelsohn was one of a kind. He seemed to be

withdrawn and moody, but he was a master at the concept and marketing of developments in Florida. In the Fort Myers area in the fifties and sixties, there were three large developments: Cape Coral, Lehigh Acres, and San Carlos Park. Today, these three developments, which were completely undeveloped, now are home to some two hundred thousand people. Milt Mendelsohn was the marketing spark plug in the sale of all the lots in these developments. For example, while roads were built, or development was underway, Milt had a sign on the barricade that read "Pardon Our Progress." I notice that today most developers have copied Milt's idea and use this sign whenever they have roads under construction. All the brochures that Milt prepared for the properties were color coded for the different priced properties and were works of art. He had one bad habit. Milt had no concept of the value of money. He spent money like the proverbial "drunken sailor."

In the nineteen-fifties there were only a handful of developers in Florida. We all knew each other, and though we were competitive, we were members of our own "club" and would exchange information as needed. In this regard, I remember a phone call from Leonard Rosen who had started to develop Cape Coral (which today is a city of over 150,000 people). Len and his brother Jack were in the process of developing Cape Coral. Len was interviewing Milt Mendelsohn for the job of Marketing Manager for his new city. Len called me for a reference relating to Milt. I told Len that Milt was a marketing genius, but my caveat was "don't let him near a checkbook." Len hired him and Cape Coral was and is a huge success.

We had started our development business at San Carlos Park in October 1954. We had tested and refined our marketing program and succeeded in our project. Now, since we had plotted our original 800 lots and sold them immediately, it was only logical to acquire more property and expand our successful venture. However, by mutual agreement with Jules, I had remained with our accounting practices in the North in 1953 to sell and liquidate our assets while Jules had gone to Florida. His job was to scout out opportunities in Florida. He settled in Miami and after a few months decided that we could profitably go into the home building business. He discovered that we could purchase lots in Hialeah for about $200.00. We could build a house at a total cost of $4,500.00. We could obtain a first mortgage from a bank for $4,000.00. We could sell the house for about $7,500.00. Since the buyers were mostly low-income people coming to Florida in search of a new start, we could ask only for a down payment of around $450.00, which paid for the real estate commission. The economics were that we had to take a second-mortgage of around $3,500.00 on each house. Therefore we had a cash investment of about $1,000.00 in each house. It appeared profitable and made business sense. We needed to find a construction foreman, and fortunately Jules was referred to "Red" Keathley.

"Red" was an interesting character. I don't even remember his real first name because everyone called him "Red." Red was an excellent builder and construction foreman. He was a very likeable "Conch." (A "Conch" is someone who was born and lived in Key West.) Red had been overseas in the army. When he came to us for a job, he was totally broke, driving an old 1927 Ford truck. Jules hired him, and Red built all our houses in Miami and Hialeah from 1953 till 1957. We built over 200 homes in this period. As we worked with Red, we got to know him and his interesting family history. Red's father, John Keathley, was the Grand Dragon of the Florida Ku-Klux Klan, a first class hate monger. Red's brother was George Keathley who was a Broadway play producer, and Red's sister was a ballet dancer in New York. While Red's father was an out-and-out racist, Red and his brother and sister were all liberals who had nothing to do with their father. One evening Red invited Jules and me to attend an informal evening in a storefront dinner theatre. It was an evening where they were testing out a new play that they hoped would wind up on Broadway. George Keathley was to be the producer for the play. As the plot unfolded for about two hours, I noticed that George Keathley was seated in the front of the theatre. There was a young man seated next to him and both George and the young man, who was obviously the author, were taking notes following every motion of the action on the stage. After the performance, Red introduced me to his brother George, and the author of the play. The author was Tennessee Williams and the play they had just performed was *Cat on a Hot Tin Roof.* Of course, they were playing these performances in order to make any changes necessary before they took the play to Broadway. Within months, the play was performed in New York and became a smash hit and winner of the best play award for the year in 1955.

Jules was in charge of the building business in Miami, and I was in charge of the development business in Fort Myers. While the building business was profitable, it was taking all the cash generated by the development sales. This cash was being used in the building business to, in effect, produce second mortgages. I was running the field developments, and I needed more money to buy and develop property. That was where we were making the real cash profits. Jules and I agreed to terminate the building business. In addition to the savings in cash, Jules needed to devote more time to our profitable development business. I was traveling to Ft. Myers twice a week by car, six hours traveling each day, spending three days a week on all phases of the development—the planning, physical construction of roads, canals, land clearing, etc. We had built our own office building in Coral Gables. Jules operated mainly from that office, in charge of all ongoing activities and most importantly, our advertising and marketing programs.

As we purchased additional land and developed more and more properties, we needed a strong marketing program. After interviewing several individuals for the job of Marketing Director, an older, well-groomed gentleman applied for the position. Jules and I immediately knew that this was our man. His name was Rube Josephson and his credentials were excellent. Rube had been the Sales Manager of a large firm in New Jersey, had retired at the age of 58, but had become bored with retirement. We hired him immediately. He remained with our company for fifteen years until he retired.

Rube's sales background was impeccable. As a young lad he had obtained a job as an apprentice to a "medicine man." In the late 1800's and into about the early 1900's, there were salesmen who went from town to town, in the early days by wagon, and later by truck. They would stop in a small town, round up a crowd, and sell all kinds of medicines and medicinal products from their vehicle. Usually they employed a "shill" to liven up the crowd and help with the sales. Rube, as a "shill" had apprenticed himself to one of these "snake charmers." In this milieu, he excelled in sales promotion. As he became older, he held many important sales positions. In the early 1930s, John McArthur, who was starting to make a fortune in the insurance business in Chicago, hired him. McArthur was operating several insurance companies, had a large sales force, and sold low-cost life insurance policies. His largest company, White Cross Insurance Co., was a gold mine. While the company sold life insurance, they rarely paid off any claims since, at the bottom of every policy, there was a statement in small print that stated "to authenticate a death claim, the body must be delivered to the main office in Texas." Rube said that John McArthur was an awful person, mean, avaricious, and selfish. John's brother was Charles McArthur, the prominent New York playwright who was married to Helen Hayes, the actress. Charles would have nothing to do with his brother John. Rube's job with White Cross Insurance was rock solid, and he could have stayed on comfortably for many years. However, Rube did not like the phony tactics employed by John McArthur, so he left the company.

John McArthur later became a multi-billionaire. When he died he left many billions of dollars in a "John McArthur Fund." John McArthur was the cheapest, most despicable man I ever met. He made a great deal of money by investing in Florida real estate, mostly by buying developments from people in distress, or financing developers and foreclosing on their business. I must now tell you of my own personal experience with John McArthur. McArthur had a real estate man, Irving Miller, who in effect, was his "go-fer." McArthur used Irving to find business opportunities and present them to him. Miller would meet with McArthur several times a week and bring him new deals. Irving told me that at all their meetings, the first thing that McArthur would ask is "Irv, how can we make some big bucks today?" This from a multi-billionaire! I had a business real estate deal and Irving set up an appointment for me to meet McArthur. McArthur had purchased the old, largest hotel on Singer Island. He conducted his business at a rear table in the spacious cafeteria of the hotel. I arrived for the meeting at 9:30 A.M., greeted Mr. McArthur at the rear table. McArthur called the waitress and asked if I wanted a cup of coffee. I had been traveling for two hours and coffee would be fine. McArthur called the waitress. "Mabel, bring Mr. Freeman a cup of coffee." We discussed our business and as I was leaving about 45 minutes later. McArthur called the waitress and said "Mabel, give Mr. Freeman a check." I should have kept that check as a testimony to the twisted, mean and penurious mind of John McArthur. However, I paid the 15 cents he had billed me for the coffee. That was the price of coffee at that time.

Rube Josephson turned out to be an exceptional sales manager. As our business grew, he hired additional salesmen. Rube knew exactly how to handle them, understood completely the psychology of each salesperson. Rube explained that every salesman needs "wrinkles in his belly." Each salesman has his own sales technique, but invariably, after he has a good sales streak and makes money, he spends it or gambles it away. Only then does he come back to replenish his larder. For example, we had one salesman, Murray Richards, who was a phone salesman. He would come in every evening at about 7:30 P.M. and make several phone calls, selling property on the phone. He averaged about $300.00 commission on each sale. Because he was an excellent phone salesman, he invariably sold three or four properties in an hour and a half. He departed at 9:00 P.M. I often spoke to Murray asking, "Murray, you made $900.00 working one and a half hours. Why don't you work three hours and double that?" However, Murray was lazy. He couldn't understand finances. He only worked enough to meet his needs. He lived on Miami Beach and preferred to hang around the beach, tan and swim all day, a real beach bum.

Although I had an accounting background, I was totally unfamiliar with sales programs and tactics. Rube was a great teacher. I learned marketing expressions like "backing in the hearse" where the insurance salesman shows how necessary it is for the prospect to purchase the policy and how catastrophic it would be to the insurance purchaser's wife and children if the prospect were to die uninsured. Rube held sales meetings every week with the sales staff. In advance, he would paste a $20.00 bill below every chair. After the salesmen sang the company song, Rube instructed each salesman to turn over his chair. To their amazement, all the salesmen found a $20.00 bill. Rube would say "See fellows, if you get off your ass, you can make a lot of money."

However, I was spending three days a week in Ft. Myers at our San Carlos Park development. The trip from Coral Gables, where I lived was over three hours by auto. Our development business was booming. I was buying additional land adjacent to our property and planning, clearing, building roads, canals, etc. I was learning and becoming a successful developer on the Southwest Coast of Florida.

Author's first field office at San Carlos Park in 1955.

CHAPTER SIX

LAND DEVELOPMENT FOR BEGINNERS

In October 1954, I began driving through the Florida Everglades from Miami to Ft. Myers. For the next nine years, I drove twice a week through this pristine jungle to get to my development, San Carlos Park. At this time, in 1954, the development was just a 240 acre untamed wilderness. It was my job to create a city; develop lots for sale to the public; build parks, lakes, and other facilities. It was an awesome job for a young man, born and bred in the New York area, suddenly required to become a developer. However, as a good businessman and with an accounting background, I was sure I could accomplish the job. I always believed that any businessman, who could successfully run a candy store, could also run General Motors, because the business principles were identical.

I drove on the old Tamiami Trail which was constructed in the early nineteen hundreds. It cut a swath westerly through the southern end of the Everglades. This narrow two-lane road had been a miracle of road construction. Without sophisticated road building equipment, using horses and mules to pull ancient graders and dozer blades, using old steam shovels to dig the canals necessary to build the road, this was a construction miracle. On each side of the road, 50-foot canals had been dug to both drain the road and to provide the fill for the roadbed. As I drove along, I often saw big alligators sunning themselves on the canal banks, and otters swimming in the canals or occasionally darting across the road in front of my car. Once when I swerved to avoid hitting one of these creatures, I almost wound up in the canal. At certain times of the year, a particular area of the road would have hundreds of snakeskins, which the rattlesnakes had shed as they grew. I was especially wary of the black vultures, nature's garbage collectors. They ate the road-killed animals. After losing several windshields from hitting a vulture too full of food to take off the pavement, whenever I saw these ugly creatures feasting on the road, I would slow down and sound my horn to scare them out of my way.

After the long three and one-half hour trip from Miami to Ft. Myers, I finally would arrive at my land project. I looked at the 240 acres of sheer wilderness and wondered how to start the transformation of this weed-strewn area into a successful subdivision. I was a big-city young man from New York and New Jersey. To begin, I had to learn my new occupation from the local inhabitants. Fortunately, I engaged the best engineering firm in the town, Carl Johnson Engineering Company. Together with Carl, I spent many hours going over the maps and terrain that was involved, and I appreciated that Carl was a real environmentalist. He suggested that we leave park areas, canals and lakes on the property so that the future residents would have open spaces and the development would be successful. As any developer knows, a well-planned community engineered with environmental concerns is not only a good project for the future residents, but it also essential to having a profitable and successful community.

My next step was to employ local people to do the actual development; operate the heavy equipment machines that I had to purchase. Fort Myers was a small town at that time in the 1950's, so I found most of my employees lived in Immokalee, a farming community about twenty miles east of town. Immokalee was on the western edge of the Everglades, and being in a remote area adjoining the Everglades, the inhabitants were hard working, agricultural workers familiar with all farm and heavy equipment. I was amazed to find that these untutored people; living in this remote area and getting almost all of their food and sustenance from the plentiful game in the area respected and preserved all the natural beauty of the adjacent Everglades.

The people who talk about the Everglades usually reside in big cities, attend prestigious colleges and get a degree of some sort that classifies them as "Environmentalists." I venture to say that if they rode through the Everglades as often as I did and later flew over it almost daily in my plane, they would have a better understanding of this unique area. Yet, this country has unfortunately, for political purposes, designated these neophytes to "cure" an area where they never lived and with which they are unfamiliar. The young Southern people that I employed from Immokalee lived in an area where there was almost no employment. They lived off the land. They had little money, but they lived well. There were plenty of deer, wild hogs, turtles and other sources of food. Their "chickens" were plentiful. They would catch a large wading bird, snap its neck and have a delicious chicken-type dinner. Alligator tails were another gourmet item. I still own a 200-acre farm in this area with deer, wild turkeys, wild hogs, and quail in the woods, and lakes full of fish and alligators. If I wanted to solve any environmental problems in the Everglades, the native people who live in this area would be my choice as designated "Environmentalists." They have the native "smarts" that cannot be learned in college.

The Tamiami Trail ran from Miami to Tampa, Florida. Twice a week, I drove across the "Trail" and ninety miles from Miami I arrived at a small fishing village called Naples, on the Gulf of Mexico. I would estimate that in 1954, and for a few years thereafter, the residents numbered about 200. Today, Naples and the surrounding areas are all developed. The latest 2000 census counted over 260,000 people now living in Collier County. Many homes on the Gulf sell for five million and up. I have been told that Stephen Spielberg, the famous Hollywood producer, has bought several Gulf front lots in Naples and is building a huge home, reportedly to cost about 50 million dollars. North from Naples, Ft. Myers is 45 miles away. It is an additional 150 miles from Ft. Myers to Tampa.

We named our development San Carlos Park. I could easily have called it "Freeman Park." However, we wanted to name the property in relation to the surrounding area. I must honestly state that I personally have no mechanical ability. My three children recognize this. They are wary when I offer to fix anything. I call a mechanic to replace a light bulb! And so here I was, undertaking a development that required a detailed understanding of land clearing, canal construction, road building, even bridge building. Fortunately, I hired competent people who lived in the area. They were brilliant in their knowledge of the problems, the solutions required, and their ability to operate and repair equipment. Originally I had hired outside contractors. However I soon realized that I could not efficiently or economically do the job with contractors. After one contractor built one mile of shell road, worked two days and charged me $3,000.00, I determined to be my own contractor, buy the equipment and hire the people to do the job. Almost all of the native inhabitants were unemployed because there was no industry in the area. Most of the land was occupied and owned by backwoods cattle ranchers. I hired three "country boys" and started my development construction career. Originally, we had no equipment, so at first, they hacked away at the palmettos, small trees and other growth with machetes. Meanwhile I went on an equipment—buying expedition. I asked my employees which equipment we needed. They told me that we required a bulldozer for clearing, a grader for grading roads, and a dragline for digging canals. Buying new equipment was out of the question, because the prices were astronomical, beyond my budget. However, I was able to find lots of used equipment that could be purchased for a much lower price and would adequately serve our purposes. After a time, I also discovered that equipment auctions were held every few months in Florida and adjoining areas. Over the next twenty years, I bought almost all of our equipment at these auctions.

Before long, with the help of my employees, I was a successful developer. I could build roads, dig canals, design land areas, and create lakes and service facilities. Occasionally there were construction problems that needed professional solutions, consultations with engineers. However I was happily surprised to discover that my crew was competent to solve most of these problems. For example, when I purchased land adjoining my development, a bridge to cross a canal was necessary to get to the new land. I called my crew together and we surveyed the area where the bridge was needed. I asked for suggestions about how to bridge the canal. I explained that I only had a limited amount of money available for the construction. We needed to construct the bridge "on the cheap." One of the men, George, spoke up. He said, "Jack, I can build the bridge. I built one for another developer in Naples." He gave me a list of required material. I told George "Okay, you can build the bridge with the crew, but only on one condition. When the bridge is completed, you will be the first to cross the bridge, riding on your D-8 Caterpillar bulldozer." My crew built the bridge and George crossed the span at the controls of our multi-ton bulldozer to the cheers of the entire crew!

In drawing the plat of the development, I had to name hundreds of streets. Usually, in naming, established patterns are followed. First you name streets alphabetically after trees, starting with "Acorn Road." Then you go either to Presidents, states, animals, etc. naming all roads in alphabetical order. I very wisely chose as my development engineer a gentleman named Carl Johnson. Carl was a very knowledgeable person. He was the premier engineer in the area, highly respected by the county commissioners and the government agencies. Incidentally, many years later, when Carl died, they named the Carl Johnson Park in Lee County in his honor. Carl was a true "environmentalist." He and I together planned our development. At Carl's suggestion, we left many areas as parks and lakes. Even today, I am proud of all that we left in a natural state. There is a large area in San Carlos Park that is a cypress head—a beautiful natural area with many age-old cypress trees. At Carl's suggestion, we built a large lake around the area and built a small pedestrian bridge crossing the canal into the lovely cypress hammock. We even placed little signs on the different trees, identifying the varieties. Today, our development is complete. With thousands of homes, I imagine that people cross the bridge and picnic in this beautiful natural area. I don't know who called this to the attention of Lady Bird Johnson, the President's wife. However, I was pleased to receive a letter from her praising us for "environmental" concerns relating to our cypress park.

San Carlos Park grew rapidly. Our sales program was very successful. Jules and I just kept buying as much adjacent land as we could acquire, expanding our budding city. Today in year 2003, I estimate that more than 25,000 people are living in the San Carlos Park area.

I loved my work. I was no longer a kid, playing with construction toys. I was building a real city. We cleared the land, built the roads and canals and saw the untamed land become useful for people to build homes and enjoy their lives. I think people have as many rights as animals do. I know that this is a no-no for our "environmentalists." However, environmentalists all live in homes that were built by developers. They drive automobiles, use the roads and eat the food and fruit grown for them by developers and farmers. They enjoy the fruits of civilization, but they want to deny these fruits to everyone else. They castigate industrialists, developers, and farmers, but use all the amenities provided for them by those hard-working people. The only true environmentalist I respect is a "homeless, starving individual, riding a bicycle." If that individual rails against society, he is not a hypocrite! As for me, I had a real joyful sense of accomplishment as I saw our little area grow into a community. People constructed nice homes on affordable lots that cost only a few thousand dollars. We had made that possible for these average working class folks.

I spent three days a week working in Ft. Myers. I usually made a schedule of things I had to do, people I had to see, etc. There was a small Southern style diner-type restaurant in downtown Ft. Myers called the "Snack House." Everyone who was anybody in town dined at the Snack House; lawyers, politicians, doctors, and assorted businessmen all congregated and conducted their business over breakfast. I always started my day with breakfast at the Snack House. I concluded most of my daily business by "table hopping." I met several real estate people there. They always were trying to sell me various properties. I was always busy at the development during the day. In the evenings I stayed at various motels. Often in the evenings, I would ride over to Ft. Myers Beach on the Gulf of Mexico, walk the beautiful beach, and watch the moon over the calm, Gulf waters. Ft. Myers Beach today is completely populated with thousands of people. At that time (1954-1959) the beach resembled an unpopulated south sea island. In the 1950's a large fleet of shrimp boats was headquartered at Ft. Myers Beach. In the evenings, the shrimpers would frequent the only two beachside bars. I would have a few beers in one bar, walk down the moonlit beach for a quarter of a mile, stop in the other bar, have a few more beers and return to my motel. All my life I had dreamed of being a "beachcomber." I recall a movie in which Charles Laughton is living on a South Seas isle. He plays piano in the evening at the beachside bar and spends his days lolling on the beach. To me, this was Nirvana. I knew that being a beachcomber was not my fate; however, those delightful evenings on Ft. Myers Beach, walking the beach in the moonlight was pretty close to achieving this blessed state.

Real estate people were constantly trying to sell me properties. I was interested in many of their proposals because land was very reasonable at that time. In addition to the land I purchased for our development, I had some personal savings. My brother Jules also had funds available. As I found some parcels that I deemed suitable for investment, I would propose these to Jules and we would buy the properties that I had located. Since Jules was my brother and my partner, I felt it was only proper to share with him any good deals I located. I found 1,000 acres on Pine Island which we purchased for $45,000.00 ($45.00 per acre.) One of the real estate brokers I met, Susan Youngblood, turned out to be a real find. She introduced me to her "boyfriend" V.H. Osborne, who owned vast amounts of properties ranging from Naples to Tampa. In checking the Lee County records of landholders, I saw V.H. Osborne's name all over the county

ownership records. I bought many pieces of property from old
V.H., and I must tell you his story.

V. H. Osborne was an interesting individual. He owned
literally dozens of valuable tracts of property stretching from
Naples to Tampa. V.H. and I became good friends. He was a
recluse who lived in a wooden, two-room shack in Tampa, a
real miser. In fact, I heard that V.H. had always wanted a new
Cadillac, but despite his wealth, refused to spend the money.
When I purchased one property from him, I marched him
down to the local Cadillac dealer and, with the down payment
I owed him, $6,000.00, I bought him his first new Cadillac.
On another of my visits to his shack in Tampa, I sat on an old
broken sofa in the living room. The springs were coming out
of the seat. I heard his wife begging him for a new sofa. But
old miser V.H. would not spring for the sofa. When V.H.
died, several years later, he left all his money to the Salvation
Army in Tampa, some 50 million dollars.

Here is the interesting story of V.H.'s background. He
originally came from Texas. He was a land attorney, hired by
Gulf Oil Co. in the 1930's to come to the West Coast of Florida
to buy oil leases from the landowners. Oil had been discovered
in the Gulf of Mexico and the oil companies were sure that the
oil extended from the Gulf into the southern Florida peninsula.
V.H. spent the next ten years accumulating oil leases for the
company. Almost all the land in Southwest Florida consisted of
large cattle ranches, which were upwards of a few thousand acres.
V.H. was authorized to offer these owners the following deal:
The company required a ten-year oil lease and would pay the
landowner 50 cents per acre per year for this lease. Often the
landowner would tell V.H., "Instead of the 50 cents, give me
$1.00 per acre and I'll sell you the land." In the 1930s that was
the going price for large tracts of land in Southwest Florida. So
V.H. paid the $1.00 per acre and acquired large property holdings
in this area. He pocketed the 50-cent lease money every year. By
receiving the lease money, in one year, he obtained the property
for free! In the 1950s, I was buying as many properties as I could

afford to purchase from him. I was paying him $100.00 per acre. I have resold most of this land for many times that sum.

One day, Jules and I received an urgent call from Lee Ratner, who had become a friend, and had assisted us in the marketing of our development. Lee was a very wealthy businessman. He had purchased 10,000 acres in east Lee County and was developing the property into Lehigh Acres. The *Miami Herald* was publishing page-long articles castigating the developers who were transforming the wild Florida land into habitable lots. These stories, mostly untrue, and certainly, in retrospect, totally without foundation, still sold a lot of newspapers. They had zeroed in on Lee Ratner and Lehigh Acres. Lee was not one to shy from publicity. Accordingly, he placed a full-page ad in a Northern newspaper, advertising his development. Part of the ad displayed two sketches of homes he was purportedly building on the property, one selling for $5,900, another for $6,900. One day, we received an urgent call from Lee insisting that we meet him at Lehigh Acres right away. At our meeting, he informed us that he needed two houses built immediately. Lee knew that, at that time, we were building houses in Miami. We asked, "What's the rush?" From his jacket pocket, Lee pulled out two checks, one for $5,900 and another for $6,900. Two people had ordered the houses from the ad, had cut out the sketches of the homes they wanted and had sent checks in full for their homes! This was unbelievably amazing—ordering a house through the mail from a sketch and sending a check in full payment. Lee insisted that the houses needed to be built immediately or else he would be in huge trouble. We assured Lee that we would build the houses and get him "off the hook." Each house actually cost around $3,000. We billed Lee only for the cost of the homes. He was a good, and helpful friend to us.

I spent many hours and days driving from Miami to Ft. Myers. Driving through the Everglades, traffic-free, I constantly exceeded the speed limit. About 70 miles from Miami, in a little town called Chocalotchee, there was one policeman whose job was issuing traffic tickets. His job was to collect enough traffic fines to support the entire town. I guess he picked on me as the poster boy for speeders. After enriching the town with a few $50 fines, I decided that evasive action was necessary. Ft. Myers at that time was a small Southern city. Almost everyone was familiar with the work I was doing, and besides spending a lot of time, I was also spending a lot of money in town. The sheriff of Lee County was Flanders "Snag" Thompson, a genial Southern lawman who knew everyone in the county. He was responsible for law and order. Like the typical Southern lawman at that time, he knew all the decent citizens. He also knew the troublemakers, the drunks, the petty thieves, etc. Saturday night was trouble night. Accordingly, every Saturday afternoon, ole Snag would round up the trouble makers, put them in the "cooler" for the night, give them a good meal and return them to the streets on Sunday afternoon.

I approached Snag and informed him that in our community at San Carlos Park we had some 200 houses and we were increasingly having vandalism problems. Snag asked, "Jack, how many deputy sheriffs would help?" I said about two would do the job. Snag said, "Raise your right hand." He gave me the oath of office, made me a Lee County Deputy; gave me a small golden sheriff's badge and two large golden sheriff's insignia which I placed on the front door panels of my car. This solved the ticket problem. However, the downside to this situation was that any time I was in Miami or traveling through Florida in my vehicle, invariably a police officer would stop to chat and invite me down to the station for coffee. After a few years, I kept the badge but took the sheriff's emblems off the auto.

To develop our property, I hired three employees and purchased the equipment they required: a bulldozer, a road grader, and a dragline. Because I was at the property for only three days a week, the employees did not have continuous supervision. I noticed that two of the three men were not producing much work. However, one of the employees, Charley McClelland, a young man just eighteen years old, was always working diligently. He was the dragline operator, digging canals with great speed, skill, and accomplishment. Sometimes, I put him on the dozer or the grader, and he was equally adept on that equipment. I fired the two sub-standard workers and made Charley the foreman. I asked him to take over all the development work, hiring whomever he needed to get the job done. Charley McClelland was a real find and an excellent foreman. I was sort of a father figure to him. We became good friends. He remained in the employ of my company for the next twenty years.

At San Carlos Park, over a period of five years, we built more than 15 miles of road, dug 10 miles of canals, and built several small lakes. In 1970, we decided to build an 18-hole golf course. After the plans were drawn, we put the construction job for the course out to bid. The contract bid prices were quoted at hundreds of thousands of dollars. I decided that again, as before, I would do the job with my own crew. At that time, I was constructing our huge 37 square mile orange grove at Joshua in Arcadia, Florida. We were operating about 20 heavy equipment machines, bulldozers, draglines, graders, etc. I had also purchased at auction a mammoth 25-yard self-loading pan that could move large quantities of fill from one location to another. I called Charley McClelland and told him to transfer the necessary equipment to San Carlos Park. Five pieces of construction equipment arrived and completed the golf course construction in three weeks. We had saved a few hundred thousand dollars by doing the job ourselves. We moved thousands of tons of fill, constructed several lakes, hills, canals, following the plans to completion. We did all the construction work, but did not plant the grass. Professional golf course turf planters always perform the grass planting.

We had been very successful both in the construction and marketing of our development. Accordingly, when we found 1,000 acres in Bonita Springs, about five miles south of San Carlos Park, we purchased that property and planned a subdivision of acreage tracts. We named it San Carlos Estates. We also developed the roads and canals in that project. It is an undeniable fact that while south Florida is blessed with plentiful, ample rainfall, the land requires adequate drainage. All of Southwestern Florida, south of Tampa is basically flat terrain. To drain land properly, lake areas or reservoirs to hold excess water must be created. Furthermore, it is imperative that a positive outfall canal be built to permit the overflow from these lakes and reservoirs to drain into its final destination—a stream or river. When I tried to drain San Carlos Estates, we discovered that U.S. 41, the Tamiami Trail, was blocking our outfall canal. All the water was backing up onto our property, not only flooding us but many homeowners who lived in the woods adjoining our property. I stood by the roadside and saw the lake of water that needed to cross under the Tamiami Trail, into the Imperial River, on the other side of the road. Charley McClelland and Dan Rutledge, my two construction foremen, noticed a large block culvert was located several hundred feet further up the road. I said, "Charley, dig a canal over to the box culvert and the water will be gone." I stood by as Charley completed the canal. Within a half hour, all the standing water on our property was gone. A flood of water was headed under the Tamiami Trail into the Imperial River. Suddenly, many people who lived in the neighborhood, and whose homes had been flooded for months, came by to thank us for solving their flooding situation.

As I write this, I think of the many construction projects in which I participated. These basic development projects made properties usable for people. The acres of citrus groves that I planted provided food for an expanding population. Most of this construction work today would be outlawed or impossible to complete because our friends, the environmentalists and the politicians would not permit this necessary development. I am proud that through the efforts of our companies, we have created many thousand jobs for people in Florida.

The construction machinery available today is so powerful and fast-moving that projects can be accomplished rapidly. Therefore, I will never understand why a federal or state government road project consisting of a few miles, takes three or more years to build, at an unbelievably enormous cost. We were building a mile of road every two months. Yet as you ride along a road construction site today, you invariably see most of the equipment sitting idle for days and weeks. Such a waste of taxpayer money and resources!

Southwest Florida Major Developments

1953-1970

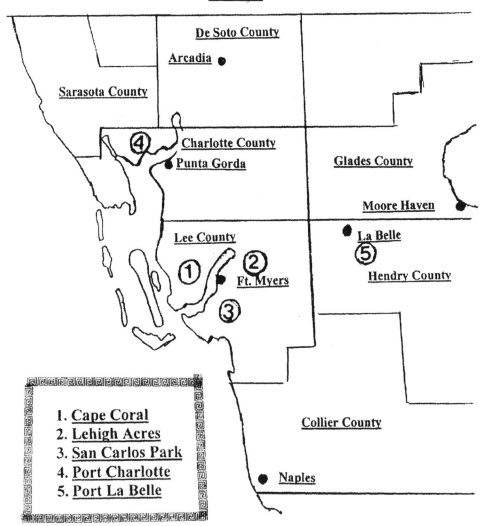

De Soto County

Arcadia

Sarasota County

④ Charlotte County
Punta Gorda

Glades County

Moore Haven

La Belle
⑤

Lee County

① ② Ft. Myers

Hendry County

③

Collier County

Naples

1. Cape Coral
2. Lehigh Acres
3. San Carlos Park
4. Port Charlotte
5. Port La Belle

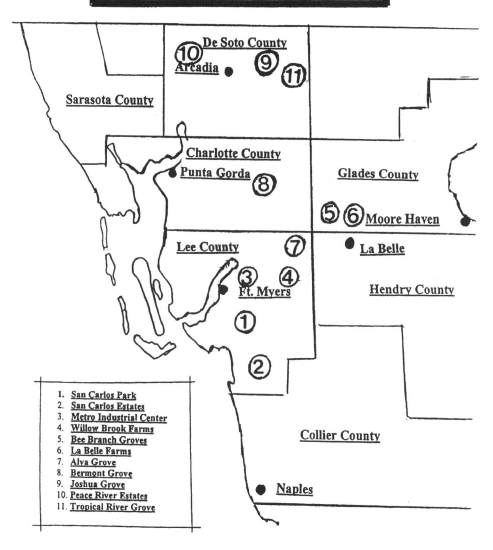

Properties developed
By the Author

De Soto County

Arcadia

Sarasota County

Charlotte County

Punta Gorda

Glades County

Moore Haven

Lee County

La Belle

Ft. Myers

Hendry County

1. San Carlos Park
2. San Carlos Estates
3. Metro Industrial Center
4. Willow Brook Farms
5. Bee Branch Groves
6. La Belle Farms
7. Alva Grove
8. Bermont Grove
9. Joshua Grove
10. Peace River Estates
11. Tropical River Grove

Collier County

Naples

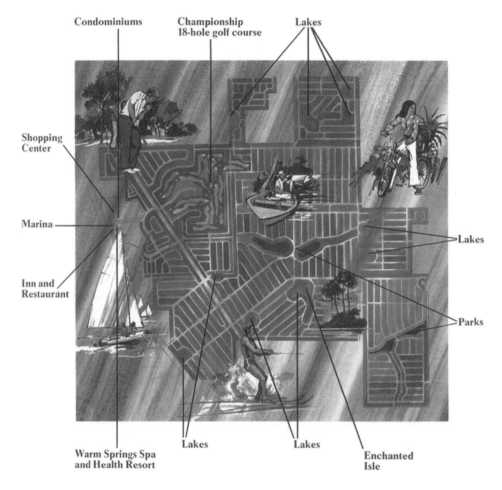

Condominiums   Championship   Lakes
                18-hole golf course

Shopping
Center

Marina

Lakes

Inn and
Restaurant

Parks

Lakes   Lakes

Warm Springs Spa   Enchanted
and Health Resort   Isle

Overall Engineering Design of the City of San Carlos Park

Aerial view of San Carlos Park under construction.

Aerial view of part of San Carlos as completed.

CHAPTER SEVEN

LAND DEVELOPER TO FARMER

The Florida "land development" business began immediately after the end of World War II. Large contingents of soldiers, especially airmen, had been stationed in Florida. (Incidentally, the U.S. Air Force built myriad airports all over the state for pilot training.) When the war was over, many soldiers preferred to stay in this beautiful, sunny state rather than return to their northern homes. At that time, there were no large developers. However, as the demand for homes and properties became strong, local developers started to provide product to satisfy the new residents. In the late 1940s, a local developer in Miami, the Mackle Brothers, jumped in with various projects. The demand for housing was so strong that they branched out into developments all over the state. Developers and northern real estate investors, sensing the trend, moved into Florida, bought the land for a pittance; developed and sold the properties to new residents. The developers noticed that there was a great demand for all the products that were unobtainable during the war. That is how the Florida post-war land boom started.

At that time, land on the Florida East Coast, stretching from Miami to Palm Beach, was fairly expensive. However, on the West Coast of Florida, from Naples to Tampa, land could be purchased at reasonable prices. Therefore, the area around Fort Myers became a prime target for developers. Before long, there were three developments in the Fort Myers area: Lehigh Acres, Cape Coral, and San Carlos Park. Jules and I were the developers of San Carlos Park; Lee Ratner, a successful business entrepreneur, developed Lehigh Acres; the Rosen brothers, Jack and Leonard, promoters from Baltimore, Maryland, developed Cape Coral Approximately 200,000 lots were sold in Cape Coral alone. Initially, lots were sold through newspaper advertising in northern states and through the mail. Prices were low and all the lots were purchased, usually on long-term payment plans. Some transactions required down payments as low as $10.00 with payments of $10.00 a month. As sales progressed, the prices and payments varied upward.

In time, the competition for sales increased among all the developers. The Rosen Brothers, who had been in the perfume marketing business in the North, were most aggressive in their sales practices. They started Cape Coral in 1956, hired the best salesmen and built a powerful sales organization, not only in Florida, but also all over the country and overseas. They developed a sales program that provided such high-cost items as dinner parties for prospects, airplane trips to Florida to visit the property, free lodging, food, etc. Because of Cape Coral's expensive sales program, costs skyrocketed for all developers. Jules and I had already sold most of the lots in our development at San Carlos Park, and we felt that the excesses of these sales tactics, besides creating major problems, could not be sustained profitably. Therefore, while we continued our low-cost sales program, mainly through sales at the property office and mailings, we were seeking another business venture. In 1960, our real estate broker, Bill Reynolds, approached us about a development program aimed at creating citrus groves. Bill knew a farmer, Lon Gleason, who owned 4,000 acres of raw land in Charlotte County. Bill had a real estate salesman in his office, Bob Johnson, who specialized in the sale of citrus properties. Bill told us that we could arrange a partnership with the farmer Lon, who would develop the orange groves, while Bill's citrus salesman, Bob Johnson, would sell the groves. Our participation would be to invest the money necessary to develop the groves. A new corporation would be started. Lon Gleason would deed the land to the new company; we would provide the investment capital and be partners in the enterprise. The groves would be sold in the same fashion that we were selling home sites. We all would share the profits.

At that time, I did a great deal of research into the citrus business. I discovered that owning orange groves was very profitable. A citrus farmer who owned even a ten-acre grove could earn enough to make a decent living, even enough to send his children to college. Most of the citrus groves were in Polk County, some seventy miles north of the groves we were planning to develop. As I researched the agricultural feasibility of planting in our area, all the established citrus farmers told me that citrus trees would not grow in that area because the soil was so poorly drained that the trees would die. In fact, Professor Louis Mayers, the foremost expert on citrus plantings at the University of Florida, said that citrus could not be successfully planted in this southern area of Florida.

I called the Florida Department of Agriculture, and at my request, they sent several expert citrus "doctors" to examine our land. Dr. Wally Long, a renowned citrus expert at that time, assured us that we could have an excellent grove if we properly drained the property by constructing ditches and canals. He put us in touch with a citrus engineer, Kenneth Harris, who had just developed the plan for the Coca-Cola Company that was planting thousands of acres in Ft. Pierce for its Minute Maid orange juice. Ken also developed a complete engineering plan that we implemented. Ken was instrumental in designing and engineering all our groves-some 31,000 acres (approximately 50 square miles.)

Since we had established the feasibility of the farm plan, its economic viability, and its overall potential profitability, we decided to proceed. We made a substantial initial investment to get the business going. However, big problems soon developed.

Our erstwhile farmer, Lon Gleason, who was supposed to know all about farming, proved to be totally incompetent. Months passed by with no tangible results. There were always excuses, but nothing was happening. Money was evaporating. Furthermore, after six months, our supposedly excellent real estate salesman had been unable to make even one sale. We determined that, again, extraordinary action was necessary. I called in our farmer and told him we were hemorrhaging money so our partnership was terminated. I purchased 3,300 acres of the property from him and decided that, despite my lack of agricultural knowledge, I was going to plant these groves and make this a successful enterprise. I moved my construction equipment to the new farm and, following the engineer's plan, planted 160 acres of orange trees. This grove was to be our first test of the project.

Little did I realize that this new phase in my personal career would create such a dramatic change. To a city boy, in the economic ladder, the farmer is the lowest possible denominator, even though he provides all the food and subsistence necessary to the existence of the city dweller. My wife chided me, saying, "you started out as a C.P.A., then became a developer, and now you have become a farmer. You sure have sunk pretty low." I did not realize that when I started in citrus development, I would eventually build the largest orange grove in Florida—at Joshua in Arcadia: 37 square miles; about 23,000 acres. I would also plant 3,600 acres in Lee County at Alva—some 6 square miles and 3,300 acres at Bermont in Charlotte County—also about 6 square miles. I also planted 200 acres at my personal farm in La Belle, Florida, and 640 acres in Arcadia making a total of about 50 square miles of orange groves, or 31,000 acres. We planted over 4,000,000 trees!

While it was a tremendous amount of work, I must confess that it was easy and enjoyable. I had a great crew, my "country boys," who could operate any type of huge construction equipment. My job was to coordinate the personnel, buy the equipment and supervise the entire operation. Along the way, having had a good background in business, I instituted several good management practices. I started incentive plans, set goals, and awarded bonuses for early completion of those goals. If my crew completed developing a certain area before Christmas, a Christmas tree with bonus envelopes would be awaiting them at the completion point. We achieved remarkable results by stimulating competition between the various operators. For example, when we constructed ten-acre grove parcels with road graders, we painted one grader red, and the other grader white. We called one the "White Swan" and the other the "Red Runner." As the workday commenced, one grader started in one ten-acre block, and the other in an adjacent 10 acres. The White Swan and the Red Runner operators would compete to see who could complete his job by noontime. The grader operator who finished first received a free lunch. All the employees would bet on either the white or red grader, and winners were held in great esteem. We were also digging hundreds of miles of drainage canals, operating seven draglines and backhoes. To keep our dragline employees from "goofing off," I had one employee whose sole job was measuring the amount of fill that was being dug. He would stake each pile of dirt for each dragline, returning at the end of a week to measure the amount of fill each machine had piled that week. Thus we rewarded the efficient operators and replaced the marginal employees. By the use of management techniques like these, and with a group of superior managers and employees, we were able to develop 37 square miles of citrus grove in three and one-half years at the Joshua Grove in De Soto County.

In 1962, I was developing San Carlos Park and had started our first citrus project at Bermont in Charlotte County. Traveling by car, I was on the road between these two projects for about four days a week. Someone suggested that I would be able to move faster and more efficiently if I had my own plane and learned to fly. Young and always ready to try new challenges, I purchased a Cessna 172 airplane for $7,500.00 and began my aviation career. My plane was called N9199B, affectionately called "99Bravo." It was practically new, having been flown for only 150 hours. Today, that same plane sells new for over $200,000.00. Cessna in the 1970s had stopped manufacturing small planes for many years because greedy attorneys were having a field day, suing aviation manufacturers with unjustified lawsuits. They practically stopped all small plane production for almost twenty years, depriving many would-be pilots from learning to fly. Finally Congress passed legislation permitting the aviation companies to resume production, protected from these outrageous lawsuits. Production of small planes was resumed, but at a steeply higher price.

Most people believed that my aviation career could end in only two ways: I would kill myself or I would hire a competent pilot. I was a terrible pilot. Besides having a fear of flying, I had no mechanical ability. However, I stayed with the program and eventually, after several months, received my pilot's license. My plane, a Cessna 172, was practically accident-proof. Flown properly and in good weather, it is impossible to crash a 172! With its high wings, it floats like a bird and lands gently on the runway, unless deliberately crashed into the ground. I soon understood that I would never be comfortable as a pilot. Whenever the word got around the old Tamiami airport that Freeman was coming to fly, almost everyone evacuated the airport and even the tower operators wanted to leave! I noticed one pilot who seemed to get the respect of the others. He was a fifty-year-old gentleman, T.A. Biglow. He was a real estate broker who loved flying and spent most of his spare time around the airport flying or fixing aircraft. T.A. was a fine, good natured, and reliable person and an excellent airplane mechanic. I asked him to fly with me several times and then I made my pitch. I asked him to become my full time pilot. He agreed and went to work for our company. T.A. was our pilot for fourteen years until I retired. He saved my life many times.

I flew with T.A almost four days a week. He also flew our customers or other company executives, as needed. T.A. was a real "bush pilot." He could land or takeoff a plane in a very short field. In every development that we started, the first order of business was building an airstrip so that we could land exactly at the office of the project we were developing. Usually these airfields would be grass strips about 3,000 to 5,000 feet long and were ideal for our needs. However, although we did not have an airstrip at San Carlos Park, that didn't bother T.A. He lined up the plane on final approach and landed on one of our roads. This was a remarkable feat since the road was only 18 feet wide and the wheels of the plane were 16 feet apart. He only had a two-foot margin of error! Despite crosswinds, T.A. always landed safely, to my complete amazement. Furthermore, when we went to Punta Gorda to work at the Bermont Grove, before we had constructed our airstrip, we would land on State Road #74, and pull the plane off the road onto a ramp. One of our employees would pick us up in a car and bring us back when we were ready to leave. Then T.A. and I would pull the plane back onto the state road, and take off with no traffic in sight! Of course, when we completed our airstrip at the grove, we landed right on our property. It now seems unbelievable that there were so few people and so little traffic on the state roads during the 1960's that we could use the roads as landing strips, taking off and landing at will.

Our first citrus project, started in 1960, was 3,300 acres at Bermont. I had taken over management and construction of the project. It was my job to begin construction and oversee the planting of the first 160 acres of grove. Our construction crew accomplished this very shortly. I also had a citrus nursery planted so that we would have our own trees available. We could grow citrus trees at a considerable cost saving. However, after six months, we had not sold the first grove. Jules and Rube Josephson, our marketing manager, developed a sales program relying on advertising and personal visits by our sales personnel. The program developed slowly but as it was refined, we sold the entire project. My construction crew stayed busy completing the construction and tree planting over the next few years. However, as groves were planted, we were faced with an additional problem: the need to find a good, experienced grove manager, farmer, and caretaker for our groves. I started an intensive search for a grove manager and interviewed several individuals without success. Then someone gave me the name of Johnny Pond, who had managed thousands of acres of grove for his uncle. Johnny was an excellent grove manager. However, he had been an alcoholic and his uncle, Latt Maxcy, had fired him because of his drinking problem. I knew that Johnny was just the man I was looking for, even though I had been warned about his drinking. Fortunately, Johnny had reformed and was "off the juice." No one else would hire him because of his problem and he realized that my job offer was a good opportunity. When Johnny came to work for us, I built a nice three-bedroom home for him and his family, next to our grove office and airstrip. His wife Mary and son Maxcy were wonderful people. Johnny and Maxcy loved hunting. Since the area around the grove abounded with deer, wild turkey, and wild boars, Johnny and Maxcy were intent on depleting the wild life population. They had about ten hunting dogs that also served as security alarms. Their prize hunting dog was a motley looking hound dog who displayed his merit by the wounds he had received in his work—half his tail was chewed off and he had multiple scars and wounds that attested to his proficiency. Johnny and Maxcy loved and respected that dog.

I was living in Coral Gables at that time, and a neighbor, who was an attorney and also an avid hunter, purchased a real hunting dog—a Dalmatian for which he had paid $5,000 because of its reputed hunting bloodline. The attorney friend of mine was an alcoholic. He was driving home one evening at 2 a.m. in his souped-up vehicle, hit a large tree and was killed. After the attorney died, his widow, a good friend of ours, had no way of taking care of the dog. She did not want to sell the dog so she asked me to take it to the farm where it could have a good life. So I put the prize-hunting dog in my car and took it to the farm. I turned the dog over to Johnny Pond, saying, "Johnny, this is a real hunting dog—it has the finest papers—the owner has sent it to 'hunting school' for special training." I said, "This dog has been through hunting college." Reluctantly, Johnnie added the dog to his herd. A few months later, when I looked for the dog, he was gone. I asked Johnny where my prized college-bred hunting dog was. He said, "That dog wasn't worth a crap! He couldn't even compare to my motley farm-bred uneducated dogs. I gave him away." This is another indication of the value of a college education as compared to training and field experience. We all have to earn our stripes in the field!

Every week, I toured the grove, riding in Johnny's pickup, examining the progress of our plantings. Occasionally, when a huge rattlesnake would cross the dirt road in front of our vehicle, I would say, "Johnny, let's get out of here!" But Johnny would nonchalantly get out of the truck, pick a shovel from the bed of the truck, and would decapitate the snake with one stroke. The only rattlesnakes I had ever seen were at the Bronx Zoo. Yet here on our farm we had all sorts of wildlife, including plentiful rattlesnakes and alligators.

When my family and I came to Florida in 1953, the state was pioneer country, similar to that in the old Wild West. Certain individuals and certain families, by dint of vision and hard work were bound to eventually become famous Floridians. In this regard I must tell you the story of Johnny Pond's extended family. Johnny was a poor country boy who worked as a grove foreman for his uncle, Latt Maxcy. Latt was the founder of what became a famous and wealthy Florida family. In the early 1900's, Latt started as a dragline operator in Ft. Meade, shoveling phosphates and digging lakes. He worked hard, saved his money, and purchased land in the adjoining area around Frostproof, Florida. At that time, land was selling for $1.00 per acre. Latt planted orange groves, and by selling his crop and using the money to buy additional land, he eventually acquired over 150,000 acres (234 square miles) of orange grove.

Up until 1943, commercial orange juice was unknown. If someone wanted orange juice, he bought oranges and squeezed. During WW II, the besieged British people and children were unable to obtain oranges or juice that was necessary to prevent the disease of "rickets." Fortunately, and timely, scientists at the Florida Department of Agriculture, in a historic breakthrough, developed a procedure to concentrate orange juice. Thus, the orange juice industry was born! The concentrated juice was shipped to Britain, solving their problem, and establishing a new industry for Florida and the U.S.A.

Latt Maxcy built the first and most successful orange processing plant. In the 1950s, the Coca-Cola Company, desiring to enter the orange juice field, purchased the processing plant from Latt, and started their Minute Maid orange juice brand. Thus Latt Maxcy received multi-million dollars from Coca-Cola and became one of the richest men in Florida. Latt's family still owns and maintains the 150,000 plus acres of orange groves, stretching mile after mile between Yeehaw Junction on the east and Frostproof, Florida on the west.

Another phase of this story is also of interest. Latt Maxcy's nephew was Ben Hill Griffin, Jr. Ben Hill started his career as a poor country boy. However, his overriding ambition, which he often expressed, was to become wealthier than his Uncle Latt. Like his uncle, Ben Hill worked hard, bought land and developed orange groves, cattle ranches, and processing plants. He also went into the banking business. Not only did he become extremely wealthy, but also he acquired vast areas of land in South Florida. The Ben Hill Griffin Jr. Field and sports stadium, affectionately known as "The Swamp," was his donation to the University of Florida in Gainesville. Ben Hill Jr.'s son, Ben Hill Griffin III, is still today a wealthy and powerful Floridian.

By 1969, our various companies had planted over 6,900 acres of orange grove: 3,300 acres at Bermont and 3,600 acres at Alva. By that time, under the directorship of our marketing manager, Rube Josephson, we had developed an excellent sales organization, successfully selling 10 acre orange groves. We had several land development projects ongoing: San Carlos Park in Lee County, San Carlos Estates in Bonita Springs, and Peace River Estates, a waterfront development in De Soto County. However, running out of product, we needed to find and develop additional land. Our company, American Agronomics Corporation had gone public in 1969. We were "on a roll." However, finding large parcels of land was becoming difficult in South Florida, as more and more land had been sold to northern purchasers. I could no longer locate the property we needed in Lee or Charlotte counties, so I decided to look for property to the north and east of Ft. Myers. That is when I met Eugene Turner.

Gene Turner, with his old country boy style, was one of the best real estate people I ever have met. Gene had grown up on his daddy's cattle ranch near Arcadia, Florida. When I first met Gene, he owned and operated a "snack" restaurant in the town of Arcadia. He subsequently went into real estate sales, opened an office on the main street and became hugely successful. He not only sold real estate, but also developed a large agricultural, orange grove, and cattle business. I asked Gene to find some 20,000 acres of land that I needed for an orange grove development. Calvin Houghland, from Nashville, Tennessee, owned the 47,000 acre Brighthour Cattle Ranch on Rt. 70, east of Arcadia. Cal was not interested in selling. However, Gene, by persistence, convinced Cal that the north half of his property, some 23,000 acres (37 square miles) was a wild wasteland, poorly drained and worthless for development. Gene arranged for our company to purchase this land for $125.00 per acre or a total price of close to $3,000,000. Over the next four years, I developed the land into our flagship orange grove development, the Joshua Grove.

A few years later, after we had sold most of the 23,000 acre Joshua Grove, I needed additional property. Adjoining our grove was a 20,000-acre cattle ranch owned by the T.L. Mercer family. I told Gene that I sorely needed that property because I was running out of inventory. Gene approached T.L. Mercer, who was his neighbor, and tried to buy the property, but T.L. was adamant: his ranch was not for sale. His father had bought the ranch for $1.00 an acre many years ago, and had made T.L. promise never to sell the ranch. That was it. T.L. would never sell!

A few months went by. I was frantic. I called Gene and told him I desperately needed the Mercer property. Gene, in his slow country drawl said, "Jack, don't worry, I'll get you the property!" Gene then called T.L. and said, in his sly way, "T.L. come over this Sunday for a barbeque dinner."

T.L. replied, "Gene, I'll come but only on one condition: that you not talk about selling the ranch." Gene promised. On Sunday, T.L. enjoyed a pleasant afternoon and evening barbeque dinner at Gene's home. After the meal and drinks, in a totally relaxed mood, sitting in Gene's Florida room, Gene and T.L. discussed the cattle business. Gene talked with T.L. about his cattle operation, asking T.L. how much time he spent riding the range, and how much money he earned from the cattle operation. T.L. said," I wake up at 5 A.M., have breakfast, get on my horse and ride the range all day until about 5 P.M."

Gene asked, "T.L., how many cows do you have and how much money do you make a year?" T.L. replied that he had about 800 cows and made about $20,000 a year. That was the opening that sly Gene was waiting for. He pounced!

Gene said, "T.L., suppose that you didn't have to work all day rounding up the cows; suppose that instead of $20,000 a year, you drove down to the post office once a month and there was a check for $20,000 waiting for you. You could make $240,000 per year, instead of $20,000."

T.L. replied that it was impossible. Gene was dreaming.

Gene said "T.L. if you sell your property for $200 per acre the total price would be $4,000,000, they would pay you 6% interest, and you would get a monthly check of $20,000 at the post office every month!"

T.L. was trapped, and after some thought, a few days later, T.L. accepted the offer. We closed the deal and paid Gene a 10% commission. He had earned it.

To complete the circle as to the eventual fate of the Mercer ranch, I first must tell you that although I made T.L. a multi-millionaire, I am not so sure that I did him a favor. T.L. was about 6 ft. 5 in. tall and weighed about 190 pounds when I first bought the property. Over his lifetime, he had spent every day riding the range, chasing his cows. He was in prime physical condition, resembling the typical "Marlboro Cowboy." Two years after T.L. sold the property to us, I saw him downtown in Arcadia. After receiving the money for his ranch, he had traveled over the world, and spent several months in France, eating and drinking well. With all this good living, and without the range riding, he had gained well over 100 pounds!

Another interesting story relative to the T.L. Mercer property is that our company never utilized this property. My brother and I sold our stockholdings in American Agronomics Corporation, and retired in 1973. The new managers of American Agronomics Corporation were unable to continue the growth of the company. They had neither the vision nor the drive necessary to build a company or develop any property. They were strictly managers. They never developed the Mercer Ranch. However, through a stroke of fortune, Florida Power & Light Co., looking for a site for a projected nuclear plant, had zeroed in on the Arcadia area. In 1975, they purchased the T.L. Mercer ranch from the company. I had paid $4,000,000 for the property. Florida P & L paid American Agronomics Corp. $12,000,000, a profit to the company of $8,000,000.

Before our retirement from the company, we also acquired additional land for development. Glades County was, and still is, a sleepy backwoods county, just east of Ft. Myers. It had fewer than 10,000 people in 1970 and in year 2003, it still has fewer than 10,000 people. Most of Glades County, some 300,000 acres, is owned by Lykes Brothers, a huge family-owned conglomerate of agricultural and industrial interests. We were interested in acquiring a large cattle ranch in Glades County, a complete Township consisting of 23,000 acres (36 square miles). I employed a real estate agent, John Knight, to work exclusively for our company. John negotiated for the property and finally convinced the owners to sell. Our company paid $75.00 per acre for this property or a total of approximately $1,800.000. We subsequently sold most of this property in small and large acreage parcels.

As we constructed the huge Joshua Grove, we had no idea that "big brother" was observing us. While we were developing the grove in Arcadia, Florida, in 1971, almost thirty heavy equipment machines were clearing the land, digging the canals, building roads, and grading beds for citrus plantings and planting citrus trees. I was at the main office in Coral Gables when my secretary told me that three F.B.I. agents were in the lobby, asking to see me. I had no idea why they were there. When they entered my office, they showed me a large photo that had appeared on the front cover of the National Geographic Magazine. From the first manned satellite in orbit, the astronauts had taken an aerial photograph of Florida. Directly in the middle of the state was a suspicious-looking open area that stuck out like a sore thumb! I solved the mystery by explaining that the suspicious area was the 37-square miles our construction crews had cleared in the process of producing the largest orange grove in the world! I convinced the agents that no Martians had landed in Florida. My bulldozer operators and I had caused this phenomenon.

Extensive land acquisitions were necessary for the conduct of our developments. Our business had grown so rapidly that we needed additional capital to continue our operations; it became imperative that we restructure and revise our organization to accommodate rapid growth. Substantial financing was necessary.

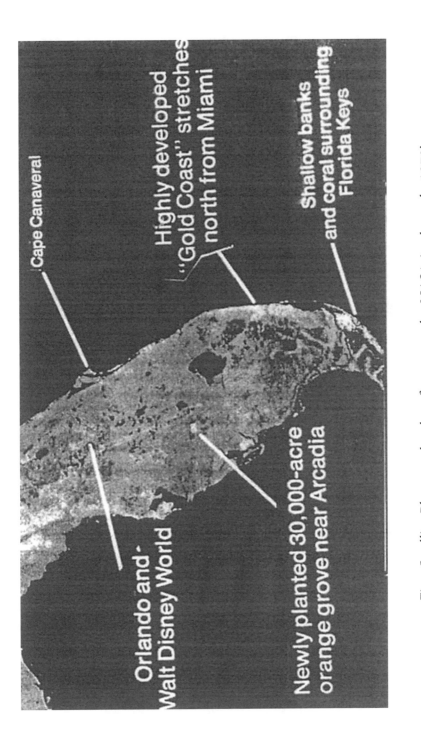

Cape Canaveral

Highly developed "Gold Coast" stretches north from Miami

Shallow banks and coral surrounding Florida Keys

Orlando and Walt Disney World

Newly planted 30,000-acre orange grove near Arcadia

First Satellite Photograph taken from space by NASA in the early 1970's.

Partial view of the 24,000 acre (37 square mile) Joshua Grove, the largest citrus grove in the world.

Another partial aerial view of the Joshua Grove, east of Arcadia Florida.

The author stands near one of the 4 million orange trees that he planted in Florida.

My country house in La Belle, Florida in a 200 acre citrus grove.

CHAPTER EIGHT

BECOMING A PUBLIC COMPANY

It was 1968. Jules and I had started our Florida business in 1953. After fifteen years we had built a substantial business in land and citrus grove development. Our land developments at San Carlos Park, San Carlos Estates and Peace River were going well. We had millions of dollars in receivables and our companies were debt free. We could have retired. However, I was still young and full of energy. Having learned all facets of the development business, I had built a great crew complete with the best road-building and development equipment. I was ready for new challenges.

My brother and I sat facing each other at twin desks in our Coral Gables headquarters office building, reviewing our financial statements. The company had a net worth of about $6,000,000. Jules said, "Jack, my half is worth $3,000,000; give me $1,500,000 and you can have the business." I told Jules that if he gave me the same deal, I would leave. Of course we were discussing this only in jest. However it did point out that while we had a very successful enterprise, it might not be possible to find a buyer for the company. In searching for a new direction, we discussed the possibility of going public. As a public company, we would have exposure to a large audience; the stock would provide marketability. Our company could grow, giving us access to financing that was not available to us as individuals. Of course, we didn't realize that, by bringing in a large number of stockholders, we were, in effect, making each stockholder a kind of partner in our enterprise. However, it appeared the logical way to proceed.

A stockbroker acquaintance contacted a New York security firm for us. Several months later, a "thirtyish" skinny gentleman, looking like he hadn't eaten for several months, appeared at our office. He presented his business card. "I'm a Vice President at D.H. Blair and Company, Registered Security Brokers. My name is Joel Fisch. I've been told that you own and manage a profitable company. If your company has earned from a million to a million and a half for each of three consecutive years, we would like to explore your interest in becoming a public company." At that time, we actually had two different operations, a land development operation and a citrus development company. We were interested in going public only with the land development company, preferring to keep our citrus company in private ownership. However, Joel Fisch saw both our businesses and was more impressed with our citrus developments than our land company operations. After much discussion, Jules and I agreed to go public with our agricultural operations. We named our new company American Agronomics Corporation. We would be listed on both the American Stock Exchange and the Pacific Coast Stock Exchange.

On a cold New York day in December, Jules and I, and several of our executives had lunch with the Board of Directors at the American Exchange. Then we were invited to the floor of the exchange, where we each purchased the first 100 shares of our company stock as bidding commenced. The stock started trading at $8.00 a share. Within two months, the stock was selling at $48.00. It seemed that the market was intrigued with a company based on agricultural pursuits that had open-ended growth potential in that area. Our growth at that time was based solely on citrus operations. However, there appeared to be a great future in developing agricultural projects that produced fruit, nuts, or other economically desirable food crops. We had enough orange production to build a concentrate plant and market our own product. There were other areas of agricultural interests with intriguing growth potential—shrimp farming, or, for example, a growing wine industry. At that time however, our main focus was the core business: developing and marketing of orange groves.

I have previously detailed our purchase of 23,000 acres (37 square miles) east of Arcadia, Florida. We named the property the Joshua Grove. It was to be the largest single orange grove, not only in Florida, but in the world. We already had developed the Bermont Grove and the Alva Grove. The Joshua Grove was to be the granddaddy of all agricultural enterprises. However, a daunting task was ahead. We already owned about ten heavy construction machines, bulldozers, graders, and draglines, but we needed considerably more equipment to complete the project. Therefore, we contracted an additional ten or more pieces of equipment, and in the next three years, we built 200 miles of graded roads, over 200 miles of drainage canals, cleared and graded every inch of 37 square miles, built a 5,000 foot air strip, built office buildings and a machinery depot at the Joshua Grove. In addition, we also constructed a large machinery facility to repair and maintain our equipment, giving us even the ability to rebuild engines. We needed to plant about 3,000,000 trees. So I started our own nursery, which produced several hundred thousand trees. But we needed several million trees. Our nursery, while profitable and helpful, did not meet our requirements. Therefore, we purchased most of the trees. In the next three years, we bought almost every tree grown by the nurseries in Florida. For many years thereafter as I contacted various citrus tree nurseries in Florida, the nursery owners thanked me for keeping many of them in business. Before I started buying, there had been a glut of trees and no customers. It appeared that, unknown to me, my tree purchases had saved quite a few Florida nurserymen from bankruptcy.

Since the 3,000,000 trees we were planting required irrigation, we imported an oil drilling rig and a man to work it from Texas. Every three days, our Texan driller would complete a 1,200 foot deep well and appear at the office to collect his check for the well. We drilled over 30 wells in a three-year period. I was totally in charge of the field operation. We had built our main office building in Coral Gables for the agricultural operation; now we purchased another office building in the Gables for our ongoing land development companies. I personally was working round the clock. I spent three days a week in the main office. The other three days, T.A. Biglow, my pilot and I would fly over the Everglades from the old Tamiami Airport to our airfield at the Joshua Grove. I would review all the physical progress day-by-day, work with our field foremen to correct problems, and inspire my crew of equipment operators working on this massive job. Jules usually remained in Miami, in charge of the office, relationships with the financial community, and marketing operations.

As our company expanded rapidly, Jules and I looked forward to a great future. We envisioned building a sizeable company so that our children could eventually come into management and continue this enterprise. When I survey today's fraudulent stock market scene, where most executives are "on the take," personally grabbing as much money as they can, bankrupting their businesses and stealing the equity of their shareholders, I admit my naivete bordered on stupidity! When the time came for our company to sell additional shares, called a "secondary," Joel Fisch urged us to sell a large portion of our personal holdings. Jules and I refused. We had confidence in building a great company. Our enterprise and stock could only increase in value and our families would have a greater ownership if we kept our stock. Accordingly, we sold only a few thousand shares. After the sale of the "secondary offering," I went to New York with our attorney and friend, Herman Isis, and picked up a check of $3,000,000 for the company and two additional checks, each for $1,000,000, one for me and one for Jules. Thus, for the first time, I became a real, tangible millionaire.

We went public only with our agricultural operation—the planting, care and sale of orange grove properties. However, we also owned seven land development companies that we had built over the previous fifteen years. These developments were centered around the Ft. Myers area. Thousands of customers were sending us monthly payments. The business was extremely profitable. After going public, we felt an obligation to the new public company since we were spending some time and effort in the land development business. So we did a very idiotic thing, costing us personally a great deal of money. Negating all the efforts we had expended for the previous fifteen years building a series of land development companies, we sold our land companies to American Agronomics Corporation in exchange for stock in the company. In effect, we contributed all our equities, land holdings, mortgages receivable, equipment and substantial recurring income in exchange for Agronomics stock. We were really naïve when it came to our dealings as private individuals with a public company. We could have, and should have, kept our rich land companies for ourselves and taken stock options in return for the Herculean efforts we were expending in growing the company. Jules and I were dreamers and accomplishers. We were building new business for the company and enriching our shareholders, but we never took one share of stock options. Gambling on the growth of the company, we watched every company expenditure and saved every dollar. We each took a measly salary of only $55,000 per annum.

Unfortunately, operating a public company is akin to being in a war zone. Every Thursday, I would get a phone call from the *Wall Street Journal* business reporter inquiring about our progress. Often we were featured in the *Journal* in their popular "Heard in the Street" daily column. Management and executives must be focused on profitably operating the business. The public demands economic performance. However, because of public interest, the financial world focuses on the company. Media attention accelerates. Every con man in the country, every schemer, every unscrupulous attorney, etc. suddenly comes out of the woodwork. This complicates the operation of the business. Addressing these distractions hinders management's ability to accomplish and grow. I must admit that I detested all the attempts by this fringe element to detract from our operational ability. I became increasingly convinced that we had made a mistake by going public.

Of course, all growing business needs financing. Florida in the 1960s was still a financial wasteland. There were relatively few native Florida banks and no major New York financial banks operated in Florida. The First National Bank in Miami, probably the largest bank in Florida at that time, agreed to loan us several million dollars to provide funds for our operations. However, one year later, when we went to renew the loan and request additional financing, we were turned down. The bank requested repayment of the loan. The economy had changed, and while the president of the bank valued our business and relationship, the board of the bank had decided to limit the amount of loans to real estate development companies. Since they were loaning substantial funds to the Mackle Brothers. and other large developers, they were requesting repayment of the loan. It was critical that we obtain financing. We contacted other banks, but it was difficult to find the funds we needed. Fortunately, we found the Walter Heller Company.

Walter Heller Company was a private financial banking enterprise that loaned money to companies based on their receivables and other assets. They were very selective in choosing their clients and researched each company in detail. They made periodic "examination" visits to assure the security of their loans. In essence they were "factors"—private financial institutions. A fine gentleman, Sidney Gruber, owned the company, based in Miami. Sidney was in complete control. When he reviewed our business, he was impressed by the scope, efficiency, and integrity of management. He advanced all the money we required for operations without hesitation. We paid a 2% higher rate of interest than the bank charged, but it was worth the slight additional cost to have a reputable company that trusted us and that we, in turn, could rely on to handle all our financing needs. When unusual situations occurred, and problems arose, Sid Gruber would personally get involved and assist us in resolving the problem. For example, we were building homes at San Carlos Park and required mortgage financing for the homes we sold. This was during the heydays of the phony practices by "savings and loan" banks. One savings and loan bank in Ohio agreed to provide us with mortgage funds. We paid them $50,000 to obtain this commitment. However, when the houses were completed, they refused to stand by their commitment. When Sid found that the bank had refused to provide the financing as agreed, he applied pressure to the savings and loan bank, retrieved our $50,000 and arranged for the required home financing. Sid Gruber became my personal friend. I used to fly him in our plane to examine all our ongoing projects. He was amazed at all the developments we were completing, and he took personal pride in our accomplishments. Later, this dedicated, 100% friend, stood behind me when our company faced a major challenge.

As a representative of a public company, it was necessary for me occasionally to go to New York for meetings with investment analysts, attorneys, etc. Our company had a special deal with Eastern Airlines, the largest airline in the 1970's. Because we had salesmen and executives traveling all the time and spent so much on airfares, Eastern offered us the privilege of using the Eastern presidential limousine stationed at La Guardia Airport. I would usually catch a 6:30 a.m. flight from Miami and arrive in New York about 9:15 a.m., take the limo to my appointment and be working by 10:00 a.m. Many times, I arrived at the attorney's office at 9:45 a.m. while the employees were still arriving and signing in for work. On my first trip to New York, a freezing day in December, I was scheduled to speak to a group of financial analysts relative to the progress of our company. Coming from Florida, I had no overcoat, and I was very cold. It was an icy five degrees. I searched out the nearest clothing store and bought my first overcoat in twenty years!

Our public company was developing citrus groves, acreage parcels, residential developments, etc. At San Carlos Park we were building a golf course for one section of our large development. We engaged a prominent Miami golf course architectural engineer. When I put the course out for bid, the construction companies came in with extremely high prices, and a completion date of eight months. I turned to my own country boy construction team. They were busy building roads and canals at the Joshua Grove in Arcadia. But by bringing down several of our earthmoving machines, we constructed the entire golf course, at a fraction of the cost, in five weeks. Of course, special "grassing companies" who complete the final project put down the finished turf on a golf course.

Since we were interested in new projects, especially in agriculture, we researched other projects such as shrimp farming, fish farms, cattle raising, vineyards, pistachios, etc. Not all our attempts were successful. We started a cattle operation, but we determined that raising beef cattle was not profitable, so we abandoned that program. We were, however, very successful in our pistachio program.

In the 1960s, the world received an ominous message: Within thirty years the earth's population would double from 3.5 billion to over 7 billion people, and the present food production would be inadequate to feed the population. Now, forty years later, this dire scenario for doom has not materialized. Our food productive capacity has increased enormously. We produce greater yields per acre on our farms, and new methods of raising vegetable, fruit, meat and fish products have been developed.

Just a few decades ago, all seafood came from the ocean or from lakes and rivers. Today much of the seafood we consume comes from "fish farms." Through the science of aquaculture, we raise all varieties of seafood under controlled conditions. In the late 1960s, all shrimp consumed was brought to the market by shrimp boats. Large fleets of boats took to the oceans daily to satisfy the demand for this wholesome seafood.

Our company, American Agronomics Corp., embarked on an aquaculture project to raise shrimp in this country.

Our research revealed the following:

1. Shrimp lay as many as a million eggs, yet only a few eggs hatch and grow to maturity.
2. Shrimp are carnivorous: the large shrimp eat the smaller shrimp.

3. In a farm pond area, the shrimp need protection from predators—mainly birds, snakes, fish, or alligators.
4. Shrimp that are ready to expel their eggs can be placed in a moderate-sized fish tank. The eggs can be removed and placed in ponds, where they hatch. In this way, they can be raised without being cannibalized by the large shrimp.
5. The cost to raise the shrimp was minimal. Fish heads ground with a small amount of corn or grain was sufficient as feed.

Since we owned waterfront property on Pine Island Sound on the Gulf of Mexico, just west of Ft. Myers and east of Sanibel Island, we constructed canal ponds for our shrimp, pumped seawater into the ponds, and placed the shrimp roe into the ponds. Within a three-month period, we had raised our first crop of bait-sized shrimp. We sold the shrimp and netted a small profit. However, in order to grow the quantity needed to be successful, we required a permit from the State of Florida for a "bulkhead line." State bureaucrats, egged on by the environmentalists, declined our permit. Unfortunately, the government vetoed a vital enterprise that could have provided both food and an important industry for our country, in addition to many jobs. Incidentally, today, the Japanese operate extensive fish and shrimp farms, similar to the one we tried to start in this country. Shrimp boats are now becoming extinct. Eighty-eight percent of all shrimp comes from Japan and Asian countries. Only 12% of all shrimp now comes from the ocean by boat.

Our company had many diverse operations. We were developing residential developments and planting miles of orange groves; we had a home building division as well as a large sales division selling properties all over the country; we had projects operating in all five of the Southwest Florida counties: Lee, Charlotte, De Soto, Collier and Glades. Seeking additional growth opportunities, I remembered that Horace Greely, the famous newspaper editor in the 1850s had said, "Go west, young man." So I headed out West.

American Agronomics Corporation Executive Committee
From left, Jules Freeman, Chairman: John Tobias,
Vice President: and Jack Freeman, President.

American Agronomics Corporation opened several "Captain Orange" stores starting in 1970: a new fast food chain based on utilizing the citrus products being grown by the company.

CHAPTER NINE

GO WEST, YOUNG MAN!

Our basic corporate business had been agricultural development. However, as the scope of company operations was enlarged to include our land companies, we needed additional properties to continue our rapid development. Accordingly, we purchased 22,000 acres (37 square miles) in the Arcadia area for our citrus operation. We also purchased a whole township (22,000 acres, 36 square miles) at La Belle, Florida in Glades County, for our land development companies. We hoped eventually to develop this property into a sizeable city. The growth of our companies was based on our marketing division, which at that time included about fifty salesmen. These salesmen were provided with leads from advertisements or referrals, and they made personal calls to prospective customers. Another part of our sales force was engaged in telemarketing operations. We opened a sales office in Las Vegas, Nevada. At the airport there, we operated a sales booth where we could sell directly to travelers. Because many of our competitors in the land business had purchased properties out west, in Arizona, New Mexico, etc., some of our sales executives urged me to research the possibility of expanding operations westward.

In the early 1970's, we were developing Florida properties at breakneck speed. I had purchased over 120 square miles of Florida land, which was all being developed into residential communities and orange groves. Because of our real estate purchases, individuals and brokers hoping to sell us additional properties were constantly approaching us. Because I had remained active in the real estate market, I was aware of all properties available in southwest Florida. The growth areas in the United States at that time were the state of Florida plus areas west of the Rockies. Several large properties out west, mainly in Arizona, were presented to me. As the land buyer for the company, I scheduled a trip to survey the properties, each of several thousand acres. One property of 10,000 acres was south of Tucson, Arizona, near the Mexican border; another property was near Yuma, Arizona; several others were in the corridor between Tucson and Phoenix. The moment I stepped off the plane in Arizona, I realized that I was personally uncomfortable in the dry, desert climate of the West. Within a few hours, in 130-degree heat, my lips were cracking, and my body was shriveling in the dry heat. As I drove around to examine the various parcels available, I was usually accompanied by a broker who lived in the area, anxious to make a sale. However, my opinion of the western area, including California, was not positive. I admit it was a personal thing; I was not accustomed to the dry heat, the desert, and the lack of water, green grass, trees, and wildlife. Not even many of the animals wanted to live out in the desert!

In some of the residential developments, there were no grass lawns. Instead, many yards had stones, painted green to simulate grass. In Yuma, Arizona, right on the Mexican border, a grapefruit grove owner took me to see his beautiful grove. As I looked at the large trees, I could not see one grapefruit. I asked the owner (who was telling me of the good grapefruit production), "Where are the grapefruit?" He replied by asking me to climb under the tree canopy, and there, in the shade, were clumps of grapefruit. The sun and climate were too hot for the fruit, so they grew only in the shade, under the canopy. After reviewing the western lands for a few weeks I still was not comfortable with the desert areas. Because everything was uncomfortable for me, I did not want to subject any of my future customers to those conditions. Throughout the West, including California, water is a precious commodity. Whereas Florida gets 57 inches of rain per year, in California, the average annual rainfall is only 12 inches.

Controversies over water are continually being fought in California. While we people in Florida dump trillions of gallons of fresh water into the oceans daily, people out west fight over every drop.

However, we did find one kernel of gold in the agricultural area of California. We met a few young farmers who were trying to develop a new industry. They needed capital, financial backing, and encouragement to establish a pistachio nut industry in California. At that time, all pistachio nuts were imported from the Middle East, Turkey, Iraq, and Iran. The pistachios from those countries were picked from ancient trees, never cultivated. The nuts were so dirty and scarred they were unsaleable to western consumers. Before they could be sold, the nuts had to be dyed red or white to hide their ugly scars. However, the California Agriculture Department had developed, perfected, and grown a pistachio, called the "Kerman" nut, which was a meaty, natural-looking nut with a clean exterior shell.

The two farmers that we brought into our company were Don Howard and Ben Newell. Don was an agro-scientist from Fresno and Ben was a young, ambitious agriculturalist. Together they had formed a small company called the Great Western Nursery Company. They had also organized the Pistachio Growers Association. Our company, American Agronomics Corporation, acquired their company. We provided all the capital, equipment, and land necessary for this operation. We started and built, together with Don and Ben, the pistachio industry in this country. Every pistachio nut eaten in the United States today comes from trees planted by our company.

Almost a century ago, in 1915, a young Japanese-American farmer planted the first pistachio grove in California. He named it the "Elk Grove." It was 67 acres and produced only a limited yield. The grove itself was far from the population centers so transportation was a problem. Eventually the grove was abandoned and it stood for years, overgrown and non-productive. In 1970, we purchased the old Elk Grove and started, together with our partners, Don and Ben, the new pistachio industry. Don Howard had worked with Dr. Lloyd Jolley of the plant introduction center of the U.S.D.A. Together they had developed the ideal rootstock, pollination process, and harvesting techniques to produce the new, larger, more meaty and clean-shelled Kerman Nut.

Don Howard and Ben Newell were fine partners. When they located 3,000 acres just outside of Fresno, California, I purchased the property. Don and Ben then planted the first large-scale pistachio grove in the United States, and also a nursery with 500,000 pistachio trees. A factory was established for processing the pistachio nuts. That was the beginning of today's California pistachio industry. When I purchased these 3,000 acres, I was sure that in the future the land, on the edge of Fresno, would be more valuable for homes and commercial property. California was growing by leaps and bounds at that time. However, I never saw the complete fulfillment of this venture. In 1973 I sold my stock and left the company. But we were pleased to have helped create the pistachio industry in the United States, spawning many jobs in the process.

Although I was born and raised in New York City, I now found myself in Florida and California in the farming business. In researching various agricultural pursuits, I learned many interesting facts. For example, most fruit trees that grow well in California would grow even better in Florida. However, because of the differences in climate and moisture, the trees would bear no fruit in Florida. For example, although date palms and black olive trees grow well in Florida, they bear no fruit. The fruit sets only in dry climates. Pistachio trees grow well in Florida, but the tree needs some cold weather to set the nut. Also a pistachio grove needs both male and female trees; one male tree must be planted for every thirty female trees. In Florida the sandy loam soil is ideal for irrigation and planting. A shovel is the only tool necessary for planting a tree. In the Fresno area of California, however, where most of the soil is hard red clay, a farmer needs a D-9 Caterpillar bulldozer and rippers to plant a tree.

While I was in California, I researched several agricultural and business possibilities. For example, I was intrigued with the possibility of establishing vineyards, eventually entering the wine business. However, the future growth of our company was not in the cards. In 1973 Jules and I sold our stock in American Agronomics Corporation and retired from the company to enjoy our own pursuits. Although my brother and I had created and nurtured a great, viable, multi-faceted company, after we left, American Agronomics Corporation went into a long, steady decline.

First large-scale Pistachio Grove planted by the Pacific Division of American Agronomics Corp.

CHAPTER TEN

GOING INTERNATIONAL

As American Agronomics Corporation continued to plant thousands of acres of citrus groves in Florida and pistachio groves in California, we were becoming internationally recognized as a large, progressive agricultural company. Therefore, foreign countries, mainly those in the Caribbean and Central America, began to contact us. They wanted to start agricultural projects in their countries. However, my brother and I had read about the experiences of Conrad Hilton with international projects and, while we had the ability to achieve many of these projects, we insisted that the citizens or the national treasuries provide all the capital necessary. Too often American firms had aided countries abroad only to find their investments either confiscated or stolen by the politicians through a change in government or outright seizure. We were aware, for example, that Hilton had been approached by Turkish investors to build a hotel in Turkey. He had insisted that the Turkish investors raise their own money. He would build the hotel and share the profits with them. Similarly in Cuba, Hilton had built a magnificent casino and hotel in Havana on the same terms: total investment by the citizens or the government. Actually the mafia had provided all the funds. Shortly thereafter, when Castro came to power, the Hilton was expropriated. Someone, probably the mafia, lost a lot of money in Cuba but it was not Conrad Hilton.

Therefore, whenever a foreign government approached us, our *modus operandi* was the same. We promised to build the project, provide employment to the native people, and provide management and marketing of the agricultural product. The only condition was that the citizens or government had to provide the capital investment. In every case, they desired the project, but invariably, they never came up with the funds. We could only guess that the politicians, so busy lining their own pockets, left no funds available to provide projects that would be beneficial to their country or their people.

The Agriculture Minister of Jamaica contacted us for a development in that country contacted us. Jules met personally with "Papa Doc" Duvalier of Haiti. I met the ex-President of Costa Rica, and subsequently, I made a trip to Costa Rica and will later detail my experiences in that country. Most notably, we met with the President of Venezuela and his financial backers at Citibank in New York. The meeting took place at the President's private penthouse suite atop the Essex House across from Central Park on West 57th Street. He wanted to develop a citrus project consisting of 80,000 acres in Venezuela. This would be three times the size of the largest orange grove in the world. Could we do it? Of course we could! The President pointed out that Venezuela was becoming an economic power. Large finds of oil had been discovered. Venezuela was on the way to becoming an oil exporter. Money was flowing in rapidly and the country was flush with wealth from its new oil industry. He felt that this wealth would continue for perhaps ten or fifteen years and then begin to ebb. He sincerely believed that if he could reinvest some of the wealth in this huge citrus project and also in an 80,000-acre wheat farm, the future of the people of his country would be secured. We lauded his goals. We could bring these projects to fruition. We asked only that the government provide the investment necessary to complete these projects. The meeting ended with friendly feelings all around. However, we never again heard from the Venezuelan President. The lesson is clear. If you invest in countries other than the United States, or in Canada, England, or Europe beware!

Thirty years later as I write this book, I can only think that if the Venezuelan Presidents and dictators over the years had invested the funds necessary to improve the conditions of their people instead of looting the public treasuries, the world today would not be faced with a Venezuelan President Chavez, an avowed dictator, friend and associate of Fidel Castro.

In 1970, when I was living in Coral Gables, Florida, was President of American Agronomics Corp and working around the clock at our land developments and agricultural projects, a friend of mine, a professor at the University of Miami, insisted on my having dinner with him. He wanted to introduce me to a gentleman who was the ex-President of Costa Rica. At dinner I was introduced to Luis de la Trinidad Otilio Ulate Blanco. I just called him Ulate. He was an intelligent, handsome, elderly Spanish gentleman. We hit it off right away. Over the next few months, I often met him for dinner. He enjoyed talking about his homeland. I sensed that at some point, he would ask me to become financially involved in Costa Rica. Costa Rica, as opposed to most of the countries in the Caribbean and South America, was a real democracy. Ulate had been President of the country from 1949 through 1953 and was renowned as the "Abe Lincoln" of Costa Rica. He rode to work every morning to the presidential palace on a bicycle! It was a headline occasion when, one morning, riding to work on his bicycle, he struck a boy and knocked the kid down—no casualties, but headlines all over South America. Before long my friend Ulate asked me to visit Costa Rica. A new president, Jose Figueres Ferrer, was to be inaugurated and Ulate invited me to attend the ceremony as his honored guest.

Ulate told me that his wonderful country was almost completely undeveloped but that it had vast potential for agricultural projects. He informed me (and I later verified this by personal observation) that even fence posts sprouted and grew in Costa Rica! I was in dire need of a vacation anyway, so I flew to San Jose and checked into the best hotel in town. San Jose was a delightful city. It had the charm of a European city and was often referred to as the "Paris" of the hemisphere.

Ulate arranged for me to meet with the young man who was the Minister of Agriculture. I spent several days with him, cruising in his beat-up truck, traveling on dirt roads. Once we left the city, there were no blacktopped roads—only unpaved roads and trails. The land was heavily wooded with huge, century-old trees. Since there was plentiful rain in these jungle forests, the trees were tightly spaced, almost defying human intrusion. The costs to clear this jungle would make the project economically impossible. Moreover, since there were no traversable roads, transportation would be another major concern. Although there was one river that could be used for transportation, the costs and uncertainties made that impracticable.

A few days later Inauguration Day arrived. Ulate asked me to accompany him to the Presidential Palace to meet President Jose Figueres, who had been president for two terms previously, and now was being inaugurated for his third term. I waited with Ulate to enter the president's office. The presidential secretary came out and escorted us into the office. The presidential secretary informed the president that the Russian Ambassador was waiting to see him. The president told the secretary to delay the Russian envoy because he was holding an important meeting with Mr. Freeman and Ulate. I felt rather good about this. I didn't mind preempting the Russian Ambassador. After all, the cold war was still on!

I started the conversation by saying "Mr. President, your honor, I do not speak Spanish." President Figueres answered, in perfect English, "Mr. Freeman, I attended the University of Chicago for many years." Figureres appeared sincere with his desire to develop the country and help his people. He questioned me about the feasibility of agricultural development. I responded that I was surveying, together with the Minister of Agriculture and Ulate, the potential projects. I promised to report my findings to Ulate. The inauguration events included a full day of parties, luncheons, dinners—all formal, white tie affairs. These diplomats obviously live high off the hog! After the formal afternoon inauguration ceremonies took place in the spacious soccer stadium, the Presidential Ball, followed by a fireworks display, finished the day.

The next day, Ulate and I flew in a small plane to the site where the government had agreed to deed over twenty thousand acres as the site of the citrus project. As I flew over the property, I could see the absolute impossibility of clearing and planting this rain forest. I hated to let Ulate down, but I was very busy with my own projects. I was not about to get bogged down in a no-win situation. I gave Ulate my opinion and wished him well. Recently, I have read reports that Americans and other foreigners who moved to Costa Rica, and had located in the country areas, developing or living on small farms, were being attacked and harassed by the native people. These people resented foreigners, even though the foreigners were helping develop their country.

Jules and I were more successful exporting our expertise to Israel. An interesting story relative to our international agricultural involvement arose many years later when my brother went on a trip to Israel. He noticed that vast areas in the Upper Galilee and in the arid Sinai Desert were devoid of all growth. He wondered why these lands were not being utilized. From the Technion University in Haifa he gathered information on soil and rainfall conditions in these areas. He felt that pistachios there would be a good, profitable crop. Since Jules and I had pioneered the pistachio industry in the U.S., it appeared that a similar industry could flourish in Israel. Jules met with the Israeli Minister of Agriculture and presented his idea. He was told that the Israelis had tried planting pistachio trees, but that the trees just would not grow in Israel. Jules, unconvinced, arranged a trip to Israel for Don Howard, our pistachio expert. Don, our partner in starting the pistachio industry in the U.S., was head of the Pacific Agricultural Service in Fresno, California. In previous years, Don had also been a pistachio consultant to the Shah of Iran. In his research into biblical times and the agricultural history of that area, he noticed that pistachio trees and olive trees were growing side by side and that some trees in that area were 2,000 years old. Jules persuaded Don to accompany him to Israel, and he related their experiences as follows:

"I went to Israel with Don Howard to determine the feasibility of establishing a pistachio industry in that country. Don and I met with the Minister of Agriculture in the Vulcani Institute, the scientific arm of the ministry. He referred us to several unsuccessful pistachio farming operations and we spent four or five days visiting these projects. Don pointed out in each case the reason for the failure. On day six, we visited an agricultural moashev named "Beit Nekoofa" just 12 kilometers from Jerusalem. A Moashev consists of a group of farms, each individually owned. The farmers share jointly in the ownership of the equipment for cost efficiency. We were looking for Ibrahim Adu, owner of a failed pistachio orchard. We found Ibrahim. He was a rather strong, well-built man, a transplanted Moroccan, now happily raising his family and working his fields in Israel, his Jewish homeland. We glimpsed his beautiful fields of fruits and vegetables. He was a good farmer. I judged him to be about thirty-eight years of age. He was very happy to see us. He took us to his home and introduced his wife and four children, ages one through seven. They prepared fresh tea and cookies, served by the polite and cute little children. An ideal family!

"The Israeli farmer recited his pistachio tale of woe. He had been given about 1,000 pistachio trees by the Jewish Agency and told that, if properly planted and fertilized, he would have a good-paying, marketable crop in perhaps four years. He tended his grove carefully, watered and fertilized, but alas, years number four, number five, and number six passed, but he never saw the first pistachio nut. By the spring of year seven when we arrived, he had abandoned the grove as unproductive. We drove by Jeep up the hill past his well manicured peach orchards to the apex of the hill. There was the abandoned pistachio grove. Don Howard whispered, "These trees are magnificent. It would take us twenty years to grow a tree in California like this fellow has grown in only seven years. I just don't understand the problem."

"Don jumped from the Jeep and walked rapidly downhill through the grove. Within five minutes he returned. With concern, he asked our Israeli farmer, "My God, where are the male trees?" Ibrahim, surprised, shook his head, "I don't know anything about male trees; I was given a thousand trees, told to plant them and that the results would be profitable." He was unaware that any pistachio grove needs to have one male tree for every thirty female trees. He should have had about 35 male trees interspersed with the thousand female trees, to provide pollen for fertilization to produce the nuts. Citrus trees, abundant in Israel, contain both male and female gender in the same tree. Pistachio trees are distinctly either male or female. Don Howard patiently explained to Ibrahim that all was not lost. Don said he would send 35 male trees from our California nursery so that in a few years after planting, Ibrahim would have a bumper crop of pistachios.

"Don explained that Ibrahim would have to wait a few years till the male trees matured. It was apparent that waiting two years after seven years of no production, the Israeli farmer would have to be an extremely patient person. Instead the transplanted Moroccan Israeli explained "I lived in Morocco for the first twenty years of my life, praying to come to Israel; in fact I really waited with my ancestors for over 2,000 years to come to the Promised Land. So if I could wait 2,000 years to come to Israel, I guess I can wait another two years to help further my dream." It was touching to understand his love for his Israeli homeland. The next day, Don and I went to the agricultural experiment station in Avdat in the Negrev Desert. It proved to be a propitious visit. The superintendent of the agricultural station was hosting a group of twenty African farmers living at the site for a month of instruction in arid cultivation and micro-jet irrigation. His name was David Mazigh, an expert on desert agriculture. He welcomed the visitors warmly. In answer to our specific questions, he told us that he had frozen some male pistachio pollen that he didn't particularly need at that time. Don asked David if he would travel the considerable distance to Jerusalem to pollinate Ibrahim's grove. Don offered to pay him for his time and material. David refused to consider compensation but within a few days, he went to Ibrahim's grove and pollinated the 1,000 female trees.

"It was early in April. Fortunately it was a perfect pollination time. Back in the United States, Don sent trees, seeds and Kerman Nut technology to Israel. He communicated directly with the agricultural authorities. Don and I were instrumental in directing the first commercial pistachio orchard in Israel. I returned to Israel in October and contacted Ibrahim. The farmer, his wife and children greeted me as though I was the Messiah. The springtime pollination had worked just fine. The first pistachio harvest was commencing on his farm. The production was abundant. It also had a 90% split ratio, which is excellent for quality. The crop was ready for export to European markets. A new lucrative agricultural product for Israel was initiated and Don and I were proud of the role we had played in this true-life drama."

The Israelis, as a matter of survival, needed a viable agriculture industry to produce food for their people. In their desert milieu, they developed the most extensive and excellent agriculture program. They pioneered the development of the best irrigation systems, and this technology was exported to all countries of the world. In addition, though it is not well known, the State of Israel has always offered a helping hand to other poor nations, especially assisting them in developing agricultural programs to provide food for their people. This is particularly true in the poverty stricken lands of Africa or other distressed countries.

The Navajo Indians in the painted desert of the United States were also in deep despair. Of the 424 Native American tribes in the country, the Navajo tribe, numbering some 200,000 people, was among the poorest. There was hardly enough food to go around. Unemployment exceeded 60%. The death rate from tuberculosis, alcoholism and suicide was staggering. Young Indians were deserting the reservation to find employment and a better future in the general community. In desperation, the Navajo Nation, spreading across the states of Colorado, Arizona, Utah, and New Mexico, sought outside assistance. Jacques Seronde, an American who had married an Indian woman, took the initiative. Having read how the Israelis were taming the desert and producing substantial agricultural results, he contacted and visited the Ben Gurion University Institute for desert research in Israel. He met David Mazigh, the agricultural desert expert who had provided our Israeli farmer with male pollen for the pistachio trees. The Navajo Nation asked David to assist them. In 1984, David and his family arrived in Flagstaff. They had never seen an Indian and the Indians wondered why a white man, many of whom had exploited them, would come from halfway around the world to help them.

Nonetheless, David Mazigh set about his task. He stayed in the Indian country for two years, leaving in 1986. In those two years, he transformed the Indian landscape. He instructed the Indians to dig deep wells, lay out drip irrigation pipe, and start planting needed crops. His first test planting was only twelve acres. The Indians began planting tomatoes, then onions. They then turned to potatoes and corn. With dry farming, the Navajos planted 3,500 stalks of corn per acre. With drip irrigation introduced by David, they increased the production tenfold, with bigger and more robust corn than they had ever seen. They followed by expanding the acreage and the variety of products grown. They started growing fruits and vegetables and put many of the idle Indians to work. When David Mazigh saw the miracle that he had helped develop, he said, "When I saw the pleasure on the faces of the Navajos, I felt immense satisfaction." After two years, when David and his family were leaving, the Navajos gave a farewell party for them, bringing gifts of silver and turquoise, handmade jewelry for which the Western Indians are so famous. When I ponder this story, I think of how Don Howard, my brother, and I, Americans, had brought the pistachio know-how, starting the pistachio industry in Israel. In return the Israelis had brought their agricultural expertise, through David Mazigh, to the American Indians. It is truly a wonderful world when civilized nations assist each other for worthy causes!

CHAPTER ELEVEN

PUBLIC OR PRIVATE—

BENEFITS AND PITFALLS

My brother Jules and I had built a very successful residential and agricultural development company in the fourteen years between 1953 and 1967. Because of our continuing expansion, we required additional funds to continue the company's growth. We were too young to retire. Although we enjoyed the challenges and the enormous business possibilities that existed in the booming state of Florida, we now had to choose to continue as a private company or go "public." By going public, we could obtain the financing necessary to continue our growth. I admit that I was extremely naïve about the implications of going public. Jules and I both believed it would be a good vehicle for growth. As our children matured, we thought they would eventually come into the company. We were honest and sincere entrepreneurs. Our intention was to build the company. I didn't understand that most companies that go public today use this method to "bail out" the principals. They inflate the stock, sell, take their inflated gains, and leave the company shell for the public. Especially as I write this in 2003, the corruption and the widespread fleecing of the investing public are very apparent.

In 1967, Joel Fisch of D.H. Blair and Co., a New York Stock Exchange brokerage house, approached us. Mr. Fisch advised that if our company had net profits of more than a million dollars a year for at least the prior three years, he could arrange to take our company public. He made field trips to our various projects and was impressed with our operations. So, in 1968, our company became a public company. We named the company American Agronomics Corporation. The stock started trading on the American Stock Exchange and the Pacific Coast Stock Exchange. The company issued several hundred thousand shares at the opening price of $8.00 per share and used the funds to finance expanding operations. We purchased 22,000 acres (37 square miles) to be planted in citrus groves, the largest orange grove in the world. The basic business of the company was to develop citrus groves and sell these groves in 10-acre parcels to investors. Along with the sale of the groves, the company agreed to maintain the groves in a professional manner and market the crop on the investor's behalf. For this yearlong production service, plus marketing the crop, the company received the maintenance cost, plus 10% of the gross marketing receipts.

Our attorney, Herman Isis, was a competent attorney who had researched all our contracts in respect to legal and security matters. Real estate transactions were exempt from the security laws. Since we were selling ten-acre real estate tracts, he determined that this exemption applied to us. In the late 1930's, the country had been in a severe depression. Under President Franklin Roosevelt, the Supreme Court (packed by the President) decided the landmark legal case, now known as the "Howey-in-the-Hills" decision. An entrepreneur in the 1930s had sold citrus grove participations in Florida in an area west of Orlando known as "Howey-in-the Hills." The court ruled that his participation contract was a "security" under the new SEC law. However, he was not selling real estate, he was selling a participation in a citrus venture. Based on this ruling, we were confident that our real estate sale of ten-acre groves was not a "security" and therefore our product did not need registration with the SEC. We continued selling our groves without problems.

American Agronomics began its public life on September 1, 1968. Jules Freeman was Chairman of the Board and Jack A. Freeman was President. We had a wealth of experience in business, having started in 1946 as partners in our own CPA firm. We were successful entrepreneurs and had, as accountants, guided many companies to prominence in various fields. Among these companies was World Airways, the largest charter airline in the world. Many of our other clients were prominent in the building business that was exploding after WW II. Among these were North Shore Electric Company and the W.A. Anderson Company, which did the electrical work for most of the builders on Long Island, including all the thousands of homes built by the Levitt Company in Levittown, N.Y. Another client was the Donno Company, the largest waste management company on Long Island. Jules and I had moved to Florida in 1953 and started successful home building operations in Miami and Hialeah. We also built a large development in the Ft. Myers area called San Carlos Park, that today is a large, thriving city.

In the citrus field, in the 1960s, our companies had planted and sold over 7,000 acres in a period of eight years. As a public company the future looked bright. Within one year after going public, the $8.00 stock had reached a high of $48.00 per share. The company was highly respected as one of the country's leading growth companies. Often the *Wall Street Journal* ran complimentary articles on the company in their financial column "Heard on the Street." Every Thursday morning, as I sat in my Coral Gable office, my secretary would inform me that the financial reporter was on the phone. I would respond to his questions. Respected mutual funds were beginning to take positions in our stock. A featured story in *Fortune Magazine* detailed the story of a group of five recent Harvard college graduates. Wishing to donate a gift to the university, they had invested in five small, growing companies and in one year had made five million dollars, which they donated to the college. One of their best stocks had been an investment in American Agronomics Corporation. They considered it a small, but well-managed company with great potential for income and growth.

At the end of year one, our booming company, having increased its capitalization five times, set up a secondary stock offering. Although we easily could have sold twenty million dollars of our personal stock, we chose to sell only two million dollars. We had the utmost faith in the continued growth of our company. With growth, the stock would become more valuable. We also believed that our children, at the proper time, would have the opportunity to join and continue building the company. Our own executive salaries were $55,000 per year. We were among the lowest paid executive salaries of any public company in the United States. Our company was gaining wide recognition in the financial and investment area. I met with Anthony Rossi, the president of Tropicana. With our citrus production, it was a perfect match to mate our supplies of fruit with Tropicana, the largest processor and marketer of orange juice. We purchased 22,000 acres (37 square miles) of land in Arcadia, Florida. We were developing this grove as the largest orange grove in Florida, contemplating building our own citrus processing plant. Other companies were becoming interested in us for merger possibilities, e.g., the Olympia York Company of Canada, a hugely successful international real estate operation headed by the Reichman family of Canada, the W.R. Grace Company headed by Peter J. Grace, and other public companies.

Researching additional areas for growth, I traveled west. Here I became aware of a possible growth opportunity in the pistachio business. After acquiring the pistachio operation, we purchased 3,000 acres on the outskirts of Fresno, to be planted in pistachios, and we started a nursery of 500,000 trees, planting the first major pistachio grove in the United States. Our company was growing and we had the expertise for expansion in this industry and others. We also instituted a new franchise business called "Captain Orange," establishing a series of fast food stores, featuring the sale of an orange drink and sale of citrus related products, including citrus gift fruit packages. These stores, in shopping centers and downtown areas, were ideal to create a ready and available market for all our citrus production.

However, regrettably, even with recognition from the financial community and media, it was only a matter of time before our visible profile produced problems. Going public presents a problem for honest people. I admit I was very naïve about the consequences for companies entering the public arena. When a company goes public, in effect it is taking in partners. A person with one share of stock immediately attains a partnership position in the company. Suddenly the company has thousands of partners. For a person with an entrepreneurial bend, it is difficult to cope with all the stockholders, analysts, and stockbrokers who have the company under constant scrutiny. Remember, the business is no longer *your* business! Furthermore, every con man in the country, as well as unscrupulous attorneys, may find your company fair game. Therefore, going public today provides no incentive to build the business. In the past thirty years, the game has changed. The CEO, president, and all corporate officers regard the company as a personal "piggy bank." They take enormous salaries and personal emoluments. In addition, their huge stock options make them partners, instead of what they really are or what they should be: employees. There is incentive to "cook" the books, increase the value of the stock and then dump the stock. It is the preferred system for the greedy executive. The system is perfectly arranged for the top executives to attain great wealth and leave the stockholders "holding the bag." As a C.P.A., I have spent my life in finance and I know how business works. To keep the stock market and companies legitimate and to restore faith in our economic system, the following steps should be (but probably will not be taken.)

1. Corporate Board of Directors are just window dressing, a big bad joke. The company is really run by the CEO and the executives. The Directors are usually people who have political connections—retired army generals, or executives from other companies. They get huge director's fees and stock options, which is their main interest. Most know very little about business, or if they do, care little, other than to get their emoluments. The entire system of directorships has to be reorganized to provide independent and competent directors.

2. Executives are employees of the company, not owners of the company. They should be fairly compensated. They can be awarded substantial bonuses in addition to their salaries for good performance. If they want to buy company stock with their bonuses, that should be their prerogative.

3. Every public corporation should be required to pay a minimum of 25% of their annual reported profits as dividends to the stockholders. This would discourage phony profit figures. Remember, the stockholder is an investor. He provides the money to run the company. He is entitled to share in the profits by receiving a cash dividend. If the executives receive salaries and bonuses in cash for their work, the stockholder is entitled to receive a dividend as his "salary" for advancing the cash to operate the business.

Of course, this will never happen. There are too many thieves and wolves in the henhouse. So my advice to anyone contemplating going public with his business is: Hit it hard! Get all the stock you can, take exorbitant salaries and bonuses, get stock options, show good profits, make the financial community keep the stock value rising, then at the opportune time, sell the stock and bail out. This is legitimate! That is how the system is set to work! As Gecko said, "Greed is Good!"

It was 1971. Nixon was President. The election race was on. Seeking a second term, Nixon was a shoo-in for reelection. He had been a reasonably good president, and had opened up trade and economic relations with China. With Kissinger as his Secretary of State, Nixon had advanced our international relations in good fashion. However, the President, being a political pro, was determined to raise huge sums to insure his reelection. He had surrounded himself with a powerful political machine. They were not averse to using any tactic, legitimate or otherwise, to accomplish their goal. The Watergate scandal was only one incident, and eventually Nixon was removed from office. As the election campaign frenzy mounted, I was one of a group of successful businessmen in Miami who were invited to a fund-raising luncheon for the Nixon campaign. The meeting was convened in the penthouse meeting room of the First National Bank of Miami in downtown Miami. There were approximately seventy-five businessmen present. The campaign expected to raise substantial funds from these, the wealthiest people in Miami. I was seated at a table with Maurice Gussman, a wealthy industrialist (who had made an immense fortune as the developer of the "Trojan" condom), U.S. Senator Paula Hawkins, and the president of the First National Bank. Bebe Rebozo, Nixon's best friend was in attendance plus a host of Republican politicians including Maurice Stans, the Secretary of the Treasury. After a pleasant lunch, I was amazed at the program that followed. Speaker after speaker urged everyone to pledge the maximum amount because huge funds were required to win the election. However, an ominous theme emerged, turning me off. The speakers were suggesting that the contributions preferably should be in cash. If checks were contributed, they had to be written in a certain way. One speaker described how the contributed funds would be sent to Mexico and "washed" to circumvent the campaign contribution law. I sat in amazement watching this fraudulent scenario. Years later, Maurice Stans, a reputable individual who was Secretary of the Treasury, was indicted and imprisoned for his role in the Nixon reelection campaign.

I returned to my office and discussed this with my brother Jules. I told him that I was against making any contributions to the Nixon campaign. It was obvious that their fund-raising was illegal. Little did I realize that it was a huge error to refrain from contributing. By failing to donate to the campaign, I had earned a place on Nixon's "enemies list." Our company was about to pay a heavy price. Six months later, after Nixon was easily reelected, the Securities and Exchange Commission began an inquiry into our company. For the next six months every facet of our business was under examination. The SEC claimed that the product we were selling—orange groves—was not real estate but was a "security" and had to be registered with the SEC. Furthermore, some attorneys in Cleveland initiated a "class action" suit on behalf of several grove owners who were our customers. We met with the attorneys and were able to amicably settle the class action matter. The SEC sent their top accountant to examine our books. He was amazed to discover that all the records were correct and accurate. Nothing improper had occurred. Nevertheless, the SEC was determined to get their "pound of flesh." Accordingly, they agreed to close the case. However, as part of the settlement, the CEO and the president, Jules and I, would have to resign our management positions. But since we were the major stockholders and, in effect, major owners of the company, we remained on the Board of Directors where the financial decisions usually are made.

Walter Heller Company was our company's banker. As soon as I was informed of the SEC investigation, I immediately decided to notify the Walter Heller Co. We owed them over twelve million dollars. They could demand repayment at any time. I called our treasurer and vice-president. I requested that he meet with Sidney Gruber, the owner of the Walter Heller Company and notify him of our SEC problem. No executive wanted to assume this task, so, as president, I reluctantly undertook the assignment. I met Sid Gruber in his office. I informed him of the bad news relating to the S.E.C. investigation. I waited with trepidation for his reply. Calling his secretary he said, "Debby, write Mr. Freeman a personal check for $250,000." Sid said that he was giving me the money, realizing that the expenses and costs of the investigation would be significant. He knew our company intimately and admired our progress and integrity. I declined the funds but appreciated that this fine gentleman was also a good friend. He had watched our company grow, prosper, and build an honest business. He also understood how a politically vindictive government has the enabling power to kill a legitimate business.

We set about the task of finding a new president for the company. We retained a prominent headhunting firm in New York and began to search for the right man to run the operations of the company. The headhunting company sent us seven or eight candidates. It was difficult to find the right person. One candidate who had been an Assistant Secretary of the Navy came to the interview with a retinue of three or four personal aides. He was ready to take over. He was unacceptable, as were most of the other candidates. As the months passed, we could not find "Mr. Right." Under enormous pressure from the SEC, we finally selected a person who appeared to be the best of the lot. Both Jules and I had enormous doubts about the selection, but it was time to move on. We selected Harold Holder as the president of the company.

We had been working for the past five years under enormous pressure. I had truly enjoyed the tremendous challenge of building the company, and observing its growth. However, I was tired, both mentally and physically. The job had been exhausting, developing 37 square miles of orange grove, buying additional real estate for our land company, building roads, engineering construction projects, etc. As an entrepreneur, I had honed my skills, developing huge projects. Even though I was familiar with my work, I nevertheless researched and took advice from competent people. However, I could not countenance Harold Holder, an individual who thought he was God's gift to humanity, someone who was ignorant of the work that needed to be done but still insisted on doing things his own way.

It had been twenty years since I came to Florida in 1953: twenty years of full-time dedicated work. I was tired. My family life had suffered. I wanted to spend more time with my wife and three children. Furthermore, I wanted to relax and spend time fishing. Fortunately, I had purchased and built a beautiful house on Biscayne Bay in Coral Gables. I had my fishing boat on davits in the back yard and all I needed was some "r and r." It was time for a change and a time to move on.

Under tremendous pressure, we had selected Harold Holder as the new president of the company. Holder had a good resume. He had been an executive with Sears, Roebuck Co. He was well spoken and obviously had a great deal of self-confidence. Holder believed that he was the ultimate, brilliant businessman. Since he knew it all, he would take no advice or guidance. He acted on his impulses. For starters, he demanded and received the huge salary of $700,000 per annum. This was excessive compared to the salary of $55,000 per annum that Jules and I were receiving. He brought in a complete cadre of executives who were his friends. They had no knowledge of our business. Jules and I were on the Board of Directors. We had a fine group of reputable people as directors. At Board meetings, Holder would propose his ideas for directions that the company should pursue. The ideas, never researched, obviously were no-win situations. When directors questioned his decisions, he would take no advice, and he never swayed from his determined agenda. He would not listen to reason. He resented any board member who raised reasonable objections. For example, at one Board meeting, he informed the directors that he was negotiating to purchase a citrus processing plant in Wachula, Florida. The company eventually would require a facility to process the huge orange crops developing. I was familiar with the facility he proposed to purchase. It was an old, outdated, worn out facility with rusted, junked equipment. To confirm my observations, I made several calls to knowledgeable citrus people from the area of the plant, people with whom I had been dealing for many years. They all confirmed that this processing plant was a worn out, rusty remnant of the past. When I presented this information to the Board, they agreed that the deal should not go forward.

I told Holder that the company should build a new processing plant right at our huge Joshua Grove. We had enough oranges to supply the plant on site. The savings would be enormous. Usually oranges are put into large semis and hauled to the processing plant, a round trip of over 100 miles. We would save this cost. It would be a tremendous savings. I had discussed this matter with Mr. Anthony Rossi, the President of Tropicana. He agreed that building the plant at the Joshua Grove was ideal. Rossi was an excellent engineer. He even pointed out how the oranges could be moved directly into the proposed Joshua plant at a minimum of cost. Holder refused to listen. He bought the old rust-bucket

plant for an outrageous sum of money, despite the advice of the
Board. It became obvious that the new management and Harold
Holder would not accept our advice or guidance. It was clear the
company was on a down slope, headed for eventual dissolution.
Moreover, Holder resented our presence. We left the company
premises and rented our own office, off premises.

Our families and we owned approximately 60% of the stock
in the company. We had built a company with huge assets. In
our opinion, the new management was pursuing a destructive
path that could result only in disaster for the company. Jules and
I were not about to stand by and watch the Titanic sink beneath
the waves. We started to look for opportunities to sell our stock.
However, it was 1974; the country was in the midst of the
Watergate scandal. The economic climate was poor. However,
when the company management realized that our stock was for
sale and that new owners would be taking over control of the
company, Holder approached us and through the use of an ESOP,
(basically a procedure by which the employees of a company
purchase the stock of their company), he made us an offer for
our stock. Economically, it was a terrible deal for us. The assets
of the company were worth hundreds of millions of dollars. We
settled for only six million dollars. However, the assets of the
company were being diminished daily—liquidated to pay
excessive salaries, perks, and hare-brained schemes.

I had learned early in my business career that the first loss is
the best loss! The company, under Mr. Holder's reign, was on a
collision course toward dissolution. Holder was obsessed with
the opinion that retired generals were the best executives to manage
various phases of the operation, so he hired several generals to
run the company. I admire generals for their ability to fight wars.
As far as business is concerned, most of them are unskilled. First,
Mr. Holder appointed one general as Executive Vice President to
head all company operations. Then he hired another general to
head Carroll Oil, a small local oil distributor in Ft. Myers. Holder
purchased this company even though it had no synergism with
either land or grove operations. He then appointed a third four-

star general to head all grove operations. Despite this display of military talent, eventually the company, depleted of all its assets, was liquidated.

After we left the company, it was sad to watch it slowly disintegrate due to poor management and lack of vision. The company stopped all marketing operations essential to the growth of the business. I had purchased the Mercer ranch, 20,000 acres (approximately 30 square miles) for expansion. I paid $4,000,000 for the property. Having no use for the ranch, they sold it to Florida Power & Light for $12,000,000, a profit of $8,000,000. Needless to say, they squandered the $12,000,000 on salaries, bonus, perks, new aircraft, etc. We had started the pistachio industry in California, a new and vibrant business. It could have yielded large returns and become a profitable mainstay for the company. However, the new management disposed of our pistachio company that was destined for phenomenal growth. Furthermore, when we built our city at San Carlos Park, we had organized a water and sewage utility, scheduled to be extremely profitable, but that too was liquidated.

The citrus business, an agricultural commodity, is subject to the whims of the market. When there is a large domestic crop, the price of fruit goes down and profitability is severely impacted. Furthermore, the larger citrus crops that are produced in Brazil routinely affect Florida's citrus industry. Jules and I had designed and started a franchise business operation, which we called "Captain Orange." We had opened a series of franchise restaurants in order to use our huge production of oranges and grapefruits. In this way, using our own products, we could maintain control of the price of the fruit. We opened several "Captain Orange" stores, similar to McDonalds or Wendy's, in Miami, Miami Beach, and Ft. Myers. These stores were stocked with boxes of oranges and grapefruits so that customers could order gift fruit boxes for their own consumption, or ship them north to family and friends. We were in the process of expanding this franchise business all over the country and overseas. However, new management stupidly cancelled this undertaking, which was a natural extension of our citrus grove production.

As I sold my stock and resigned from all company operations, I was free to pursue my own interests. I could look back with pride at our corporate accomplishments.

We had created thousands of new jobs in the five-county area in the Southwest Coast of Florida. Furthermore, the investors who had bought 10-acre orange grove tracts from our company had made very profitable investments. They had paid $20,000 for each 10-acre grove. Every year, the net returns on their investment ranged from $15,000 to $20,000. It was sad to observe how government and politics could immobilize worthwhile enterprises.

CHAPTER TWELVE

CASHING OUT AND NEW CHALLENGES

So Jules and I sold our stock in the company. Although we sold our stock for a pittance of its value, I was pleased to redeem my body and soul. Going public had been similar to living in Dante's *Inferno*, a Faustian bargain. I made a pact with the devil and had sold myself to the company. Now free, free from intensive twelve-hour days, six days a week, I was ready to enjoy life and take on new challenges. I was as happy as a kid on the last day of school! As part of our settlement, and in lieu of cash, we had received some real estate properties I had purchased for the company. The company had no use for the property. New management hadn't the slightest idea of how to expand and grow. We now owned a complete township in Glades County—approximately 36 square miles plus 640 acres in Arcadia, adjacent to the Joshua grove.

Another benefit of retirement from the company was that for the first time since we had become partners in 1946, Jules, my older brother, and I were able to pursue our separate agendas. Jules was an excellent businessman and a true visionary. He had managed the day-to-day marketing and office operations while I ran the field projects, buying land and equipment, running large construction crews, transforming raw jungle land into citrus groves and residential developments. We had worked like a well-oiled team. However, we each now had a chance to pursue our own objectives. Jules moved to Ft. Myers, stayed active in real estate and, with his sons, developed property in that area.

Since I was an avid fisherman. I had built our home in Coral Gables on Biscayne Bay and had a 26-foot fishing boat on davits in the back yard. Upon retirement, I spent many days fishing on my boat, in the bay with a group of my best friends and buddies. In 1973 the bay had been teeming with mackerel. We would catch about 100 fish in a few hours, then give them away to friends or neighbors or sell them to a sea food restaurant. However, after a few years, all the fish were gone. The huge fishing fleets netted the fish out in the ocean before they could swim down to Biscayne Bay.

So now I was determined to go deep-sea fishing. I wanted to buy a 37-foot Hatteras yacht. However, the prices were outrageous. I searched the classified ads until one day I read an ad that described just the boat I was interested in. It was located in New Orleans. I called the seller and asked about all the features of the boat. It sounded like exactly the vessel I was looking for. The price of $50,000 was reasonable so I told the gentleman that I would buy the boat and I would fly to meet him in New Orleans the next day. He probably thought I was off my rocker! Who would purchase a yacht, unseen, on the phone?

The next day I took my friend, T.A.Biglow, with me. T.A. had been our company pilot for many years. Born in Detroit, he had worked all his life as a mechanic, building and rebuilding auto, boat and airplane engines; I knew that he could help me assess the condition of the yacht.

When the boat's owner met us at the airport in New Orleans we were surprised at his appearance. He was a tall, good-looking gentleman, but he was dressed in a disheveled shirt and shorts and looked like a hobo. I began to wonder how this hobo could own a Hatteras yacht. He took us to examine the vessel at a boat dock in Lake Pontchatrain. Although the boat was covered with an inch of dust, it was in fine mechanical condition. With only a few hours on the engines it was an excellent buy. The boat did need a cleaning and some tender loving care, but I agreed to buy it. Our disheveled seller asked us to have lunch with him and then go downtown to his office, where we would sign the papers and close the transaction. We stopped at his residence, a very nice home, and waited while he changed clothes. In a short time, the gentleman came down the stairs dressed in immaculate office garb—suit and tie—now a first class executive look. During lunch we learned that our host was Vice-President of a large building company, the Gerald Hines Company that had built the Galleria in Texas and many other buildings all over the country. His office was in One Shell Square, a huge office skyscraper in downtown New Orleans built by the Gerald Hines Company. In fact when we saw the title to the vessel, the title was in the name of Gerald Hines. The owner had purchased the boat for his executives so that they could go fishing on the weekends. They were selling the boat because it was too slow.

I learned that New Orleans was ninety miles from the Gulf of Mexico, and since these executives fished only for huge tuna, they needed a faster boat to get from New Orleans to the Gulf. The boat they were selling was too slow. So I bought my beautiful yacht, and hired a captain to bring the vessel from New Orleans to Coral Gables. It was a 37 foot Hatteras Sports-Fisher, a first class fishing vessel for my needs. For many years I fished in the Gulf Stream with that boat. Since the Gulf Stream was only a few miles offshore from my house, the speed of the vessel was of little concern. Sometimes I took the fifty-mile cruise over to Bimini or Cat Cay in the Bahamas and spend a few relaxing, beachcomber days and nights with my fishing buddies.

After the sale of our stock in American Agronomic Corp., Jules and I needed to liquidate the assets we owned in common—mainly land that we had taken from the company as part of our settlement, plus land assets that I had purchased for our joint personal accounts. Since Jules had become more involved with his family situations, the task of liquidating these assets was my responsibility. I became the clean-up man! Fortunately, my son Jeffrey was an excellent real estate marketer and developer. When we needed to sell 36 square miles of raw farmland in Glades County near La Belle, Jeffrey undertook the task. He enlisted other local realtors and brokers in Miami and within a few months, he had sold parcels of land to various individuals. He converted the raw land into cash and mortgages receivable from about fifty different buyers. I worked with Jeffrey, setting up the accounting and collections program and spent many weeks over the next five years, handling the business and relations with buyers, collecting and accounting for the funds. Every month, I sent Jules and his family his share of the collections. I spent time on this project without any compensation because I was devoted to my brother. We had been good partners all our lives. But one of the lessons I learned from this experience, although belatedly, was that in business, only a fool or idiot works without compensation.

We had acquired 640 acres in Arcadia, Florida, adjacent to the massive Joshua grove that we developed for the company. Jules and I decided that the raw land could be developed into an orange grove. While this required a commitment of time and money, if the land was developed into a grove, it would become much more valuable. After having developed more than 50 square miles of orange grove, one square mile was no problem. I knew that Jules could not participate because he had moved to Sarasota, had a terminally ill spouse, and had never really been involved in the actual development work.

I arranged for financing from the Federal Land Bank, hired one of my best citrus caretakers, built a home for him to live on the project, set up an operation, acquired equipment, and trees, built a citrus nursery, and hired the employees necessary to complete the job. Since I lived in Coral Gables, over 200 miles from the project, I purchased a truck with my own funds. Every week I made the long 400-mile trip to Arcadia to manage and oversee the project.

I worked for eight years to produce this first rate grove in Arcadia. After borrowing about $1,500,000 from the Federal Land Bank to finance the project, we had repaid the loans from our fruit crops. Every year we continued to produce large, profitable crops. In 1983, a reputable real estate broker contacted me. He represented a large company interested in purchasing our

640-acre grove. Since I was tired of managing the grove, traveling every week from Miami to Arcadia, with no help from anyone, I wanted to sell. Besides, the citrus real estate market was booming! I negotiated a substantial price for the grove— $5,500,000. This was about $10,000 per acre, top value for citrus groves at that time. While this price was a tremendous deal for us, some of my partners refused to sign the sales contract. Here I again learned another business lesson: never buy property with partners. However, after applying pressure to my reluctant partners, they eventually signed off on the transaction. We received our $5,500,000 for the grove—almost as much money as we had received for selling our large stockholdings in American Agronomics Co.

There is a moral to this story. The real estate value of groves varies with the price of fruit. The price we received was at an all-time maximum high. Since 1984 when we sold our grove, prices for citrus groves have declined to the point that they are worth no more than the land value. The grove that we sold for $5,500,000 in 1984 would bring less than $1,000,000 in 2003. The citrus industry has been devastated by foreign competition from Brazil, overproduction, diseases, etc. The price we received was unbelievably good. In fact, it was one of the best real estate deals I ever made.

I learn from every transaction. From the experience of trying to convince partners to accept the deal, and from finally negotiating a fantastic price for the grove, I learned three things:

1. *Do Not Be Greedy*: When you are offered a good price for a property, sell. After you have negotiated a fair price, sell! If you greedily keep trying to up the ante, you may lose the deal and your opportunity to sell at a fair price may be gone.
2. *Avoid Partnerships*: If you buy a property, buy it alone. With partners, you may not be able to develop or sell the property. Remember that even if you have only one partner, his family, his heirs and his financial status can affect your

transaction. If you need money to close a deal, borrow instead of partnering!

3. *Timing*: In real estate transactions, timing is most important. To maximize the sale value of property, you should try to pick the proper time—when the real estate market in a particular area is growing and there is demand for the property. If the market is not moving, usually there are no customers. Without customers, real estate has little value.

I personally enjoy living in farm country—no traffic, no crowds—only wide-open spaces. After having lived in crowded, hectic New York, the bucolic life I experienced in Florida was very satisfying. I especially liked developing agricultural projects. Since I owned several hundred acres of land near La Belle, Florida, I decided to have my own personal farm. In 1980 I planted a 200-acre grove there and built a house large enough for family gatherings.

Every year now, the grove produces enough fruit to provide a substantial income, yet requires very little of my semi-retirement time. Whenever I can, I visit my farm in La Belle to enjoy nature's beauty. There are two lovely lakes on the property, and many deer, wild hogs, alligators and fish—all undisturbed by human commotion.

View of Biscayne Bay from the author's back yard in Coral Gables, Florida.

The author's 37 foot Hatteras Sports Fishing Boat moored behind his house.

CHAPTER THIRTEEN

FLORIDA REAL ESTATE:

BUY, SELL FOR LARGE PROFITS

I arrived in Florida in 1953, intent on buying land and becoming a developer. For 50 years since then, I have been buying, developing, and selling land in various forms, either as residential lots, acreage, orange groves, small farms, etc. While I did purchase some properties in North Carolina and California, most of the land that I bought and sold was located in the five-county area around Ft. Myers, Florida, in Lee, Charlotte, Collier, DeSoto, and Glades Counties. I discovered that, in general, the purchase prices for farm or raw land in these counties was as follows:

Time Period:	Property Price:
From 1890 to 1940	$1.00 per acre
From 1940 to 1955	$10.00 per acre
From 1955 to 1980	$1,000.00 per acre
From 1980 to 2000	$10,000.00 to $20,000.00 p/a
From 2001 to present	$30,000.00 to $75,000.00 p/a

I have prepared and included here a schedule of all the land I purchased in the past fifty years, and set forth the particulars of when and how these 29 different parcels were acquired. Each parcel had a specific purpose. The land was purchased either for my companies or was bought for investment. Some parcels were purchased together with partners, or purchased especially for family members or myself. It is interesting to note the circumstances of each purchase and the ultimate sale or disposition of the property. I believe that anyone interested in pursuing an investment career in Florida real estate can learn from my fifty years of experience.

One: Properties I Purchased for My Companies

San Carlos Park (3,000 acres): Developed into residential city, south of Ft. Myers: sold approx 10,000 home sites. Now it is a city of over 25,000 people.

San Carlos Estates (1,000 acres): Developed into 1+ acre estates; sold approximately 650 sites.

Peace River Estates (3,000 acres): Built several houses; property had six miles of riverfront on Peace River; government flood criteria stopped development; property liquidated.

Bermont Grove (3,300 acres): Developed orange groves from raw land; sold all grove tracts.

Alva Grove (3,600 acres): Developed orange groves from raw land; sold all grove tracts.

Joshua Grove (23,680 acres): Developed orange groves from raw land; sold all grove tracts.

Mercer Ranch (20,000 acres): Purchased this in 1972 for additional expansion of our grove operations. When I retired from the company in 1973, the new management did not develop this property. I paid $4,000,000 for this property; The Company sold it in 1974 for $12,000,000 to Florida Power & Light Co.

Fresno. California (3,000 acres): Developed into the first large-scale pistachio grove in the U.S.A.

Citrus Grove—Hendry County (640 acres): Purchased existing orange grove; the company resold the grove.

Two: Properties I Purchased with Partners

Pine Island (1,000 acres): Purchased with Jules as partner. We subsequently divided the property.

Pine Island (350 acres): Pine Island Sound waterfront property. Purchased with Jules as partner.

Pine Island (170 acres): Waterfront property, located on the Caloosahatchie River. Holding for sale.

Punta Gorda (85 acres): U.S.#41 road frontage. Purchased in partnership with Jules and sister Sylvia. Holding for sale.

Beautiful Island (44 acres): This island is located in the Caloosahatchie River in Ft. Myers. It is all waterfront, located on the Intracoastal Waterway. Holding for sale.

1-75 Property—Charlotte County (80 acres): Purchased with partners, Jules and Dr. Wechsberg. Government condemned 50 acres for 1-75 road construction and rest area. Balance of 30 acres sold to shopping center developer.

Willow Brook Farms (720 acres): Purchased with partner Jules. Split property. I own 360 acres and Jules owns 360 acres. We have developed and completely sold out 5-acre tracts and we still own some undeveloped acreage and frontage on Rt. #82.

La Belle Hunting Site (40 acres): Partner with Jules. Holding for sale,

Joshua Citrus Grove (640 acres): Partner with Jules. Developed raw land into orange grove. Sold grove in 1984 for $5,500,000.

Tennessee—English Mountain: Partner with Jules. Started to develop but decided that the area was not conducive to sales. Sold for no profit.

Tennessee—Little Toper Mountain (160 acres): Partner with Jules. Planned to develop but decided the area was not conducive to sales. Sold for small profit.

Glades County Land (One Township—23,040 acres): Jules and I acquired this property as part of our settlement when we left American Agronomics Corp. We sold parcels of this acreage to approximately fifty individuals. We acquired and collected the mortgages we received from these sales over a period of years.

Three: Personal and Family Real Estate Purchases

Metro Parkway—Ft. Myers (40acres): Developed with son, Mark Freeman, into 40 one-acre industrial sites. Sold entire project.

Plantation Road—Ft. Myers (80 acres):. 40 acres sold. Balance held for development or resale.

Colonial Boulevard—Ft. Myers (80 acres):. Sold 10 acres to U.S. Homes and have the balance of 70 acres under contract for sale to D.H. Horton Co.

1-75 Frontage—Lee County (160 acres): This property was sold in two separate parcels.

Treeline Avenue—Lee County (160 acres): This property sold.

La Belle Estates (145 acres): Split acreage into 20 acre farms and sold all these properties.

Citrus Grove—La Belle (130 acres): Developed orange grove from raw land. I own and operate the grove and receive income from the annual fruit crop.

Citrus Grove—La Belle (65 acres): Developed orange grove from raw land. I own and operate the grove and receive income from the annual fruit crop.

How did I locate all these properties? Several different methods were utilized:

1. *Real Estate Brokers*—Many of the local brokers referred their listings to me. It is wise always to use a broker in making real estate transactions.
2. *Real Estate Broker employed by the company.* We employed a full-time real estate broker, John Knight, who located properties for us. When we were interested in a certain property, John tracked down the sellers and negotiated a deal.
3. *V.H. Osborn*—I purchased many excellent properties from this gentleman. He owned dozens of properties in the area that he had acquired as an oil lease attorney for some Texas oil companies in the 1930s.

I acquired a choice property, Beautiful Island, through a real estate broker. This property is part of an island in the middle of the Caloosahatchie River just east of Ft. Myers. The Intercoastal Waterway passes by this island. One day a broker came into our office and offered this property to us. Because the Canadian owner had passed away, his estate had an urgent need to sell the property. I negotiated a deal for $700 per acre.

V.H. Osborn owned many pieces of property stretching from Naples to Tampa. I was always able to buy, by direct negotiation, any of the pieces of property between Naples and Tampa, which were owned by V. H. Osborn. V.H. had purchased most of his property for $1.00 per acre in the 1930s. V.H. owned 80 acres in Punta Gorda, which I purchased for $100.00 per acre. I knew that the government was about to build I-75 and that the new highway would bisect this particular property. A dentist friend of mine, Henry Wechsberg, wanted to invest in land, and he became our partner in this parcel. Every few months, Henry would call asking to sell the property. We had paid $8,000. I made some calls and I received offers of $12,000. Henry would not sell. That was fine with me. Later, I received offers of $30,000 but Henry would not sell. The plot thickens! The U.S. government condemned 50 acres of this property to build the I-75 road and a rest area. I handled the negotiations. Having become very familiar with government condemnations, I immediately called my condemnation attorney—at that time, the best in the business—Bill Earle. The government offered us $100,000 for the 50 acres. I had been stung several times by the government in these condemnations, so I decided to go to court. Several months later, our condemnation trial came up and I met Bill at the Charlotte County courthouse. Waiting for our trial to begin, Bill was in the hallway, still negotiating with the government attorneys. Finally they offered us $275,000. I rejected the offer, figuring that we would go to trial. Bill Earle said, "Jack, go into the courtroom and look at the jury." I looked into the courtroom while another trial was in progress. Every juror was at least 65 years old and retired. If they heard that amount of $100,000 was being offered, they would consider it excessive. Understanding what Bill was trying to tell me, I took the $275,000 settlement, gave Dr. Wechsberg $137,500, his 50% of the proceeds. He presented me with a $50 briefcase in return for my yeoman work. A few years later, after I-75 was constructed, we sold the remaining 30 acres of this parcel to a shopping center developer for over $2,000,000. We netted over $2,300,000 for our $8,000 investment, a very good return!

We developed a 3,600-acre citrus grove in Alva, Florida. Just north of our property was the Babcock Ranch, more than 100,000 acres. The Babcock family owns one of the largest timber companies in the United States. The original Babcock ancestor arrived on the Mayflower in the 1600's. He and his heirs kept buying land over the centuries until they had acquired millions of acres of land. Fred Babcock wanted to go over some plans for drainage easements. The Babcock Ranch had been draining their excess water through our Alva grove. We needed to make some adjustments in our drainage plan to allow some of their water to flow through our groves and into the river.

I had an appointment with Mr. Babcock to meet him at his ranch house, built in the middle of a cypress hammock. To get into the house, I had to walk over a bridge across a moat, because the entire house was surrounded by water. As I waited for Mr. Babcock to come in from the field, his housekeeper served me coffee and we chatted. She looked at her watch and said it was time to feed the alligators. Since I had never seen anyone feed alligators, I was interested in watching, so I followed her as she carried several bags of food to the porch. Forty feet below, some large alligators were thrashing about, making a great commotion. They were trained to come for their dessert. I was surprised to learn that the food she was giving the alligators was bags of marshmallows! She assured me that alligators loved marshmallows. So I learned something new! Perhaps I should have informed the lady that feeding alligators is a serious crime in Florida. However, no one was apt to find her in this well secluded cypress-head home in the middle of 100,000 acres of wilderness.

After Mr. Babcock arrived, we discussed his drainage problem, and agreed to a settlement. As we sat in his spacious living room, he discussed his long line of ancestors; how they had acquired vast timber properties all over the United States. He said that, in his office, he and his brothers had a photo of their great granddaddy. They sometimes threw darts at the photo, because this particular ancestor, in a fit of generosity, had donated the Great Smokey Mountains in North Carolina to the U.S. Government!

After we sold our stock in American Agronomics Corp., I was eager to keep active in all facets of the land development business. My brother vacationed in North Carolina and advised me to visit the Great Smokey Mountains and asked me to look for potential real estate investments in that area. Accordingly, I made a trip to Gatlinburg, Tennessee. I stopped at a real estate office in Cosby, about twenty miles from

Gatlinburg, where I met Lawrence Love, a real estate broker. Over a period of a few weeks, Larry showed me many parcels of mountain property. The sheer beauty of the land was overwhelming. I purchased two properties of several hundred acres each. One parcel was part of English Mountain. The other was an entire mountaintop known as Little Toper. I was about to learn another lesson about purchasing property: Familiarize yourself with the property, its total surroundings, and also the people living in the area. Because I had not done my research, I spent many wasted days and weeks trying to sell and liquidate these beautiful properties.

If my homework and research had been done properly, I would have known that these properties were located in Cocke County. Cocke County, in the past, was the premier area where bootleg liquor was manufactured and sold. There were old abandoned stills everywhere in these hills. If you ever saw any films that featured Burt Reynolds, movies such as "White Lightning," you would have known about battles between the native moon shiners and the revenuers. This was the area of the legendary feud between the Hatfield and the McCoys. The natives walked around with guns and resented all outsiders. This was their country and they disliked any and all strangers. I realized the impossibility of bringing "foreigners" into this area. The natives, living in poverty, were adept at stealing anything they could lay their hands on. Over the next several years, I was able to liquidate the properties and get my investment returned. However, the loss of time and effort was wasteful. It humbled me and taught me that nobody wins all the time. When you are facing a loss, take your loss as soon as possible. Your first loss is the best loss!

In 1973, after leaving the company, I went on a land-buying spree. For the first time, I purchased properties almost exclusively for myself and family, I was tired of managing properties for others. Land was now selling for between $1,000 and $2,500 an acre. I acquired some properties that became considerably more valuable as Florida, and especially the West Coast area of Florida, grew. I have either developed these properties, sold them for many times the purchase price, or I am still holding them for sale.

I have compiled a list of all the properties that I purchased over the period from 1953 through year 1973, a twenty-year period. The following table lists these purchases. Note that the total properties added to 88,789 acres or 139 square miles. The disposition of each property is also detailed in this table. While most of the properties were bought for development, a considerable number were purchased for investment. Properties held for investment have either been sold or are still being held for future resale.

Florida Land Purchased*
Year 1953-1995

Land Purchased	Acreage	Cost	Disposition	Sales Price **
San Carlos Park—Lee County	3000	$600,000	Built City—10,000 Lots	$12,000,000
San Carlos Estate—Bonita Springs	1000	$100,000	Devel & Sold 1 Acre Estates	$6,660,000
Pine Island Land—Lee County	1000	$45,000	Sold	$6,000,000
Pine Island—Islands & Waterfront—Lee County	350	$35,000	Holding for sale	Uncertain Value
Pine Island—Isles & Waterfront—Lee County	170	$17,000	Holding for sale	Uncertain Value
Colonial Boulevard—Lee County	80	$237,600	Sold Part & Under Contract	$5,250,000
Metro Parkway—Lee County	40	$240,000	Developed—Industrial Lots	$7,000,000
Plantation Road—Lee County	80	$280,000	Sold	$ 4,000,00
Willow Brook Subdivision—Lee County	360	$360,000	Subdivided & Sold Acre Tracts-Holding Road Front,	$2,650,000
Daniels Rd & Treeline Avenue—Lee County	160	$200,000	Sold	$4,800,000

Property	Acres	Amount	Description	Value
Daniels Road & I-75—Lee County	160	$250,800	Sold	$4,000,000
English Mountain—Tennessee	160	$100,000	Sold Undeveloped	$100,000
Little Toper Mountain—Tenn.	160	$88,000	Sold Undeveloped	$100,000
Citrus Grove #1—Glades Cnty	130	$50,000	Developed Orange Grove	$900,000
Citrus Grove #2—Glades Cnty	65	$23,000	Developed Orange Grove	$400,000
Hunting Camp—Glades Cnty	20	$7,000	Undeveloped hunting propty	$30,000
La Belle Estates—Glades Cnty	145	$110,000	Sold 20 Acre Farms	$435,000
Land-Citrus Groves—Lee County	3600	$250,000	Developed Orange Groves and Sold	$7,200,000
Land-Citrus Grove—Charlotte County	3300	$247,500	Developed Orange Groves and Sold	$6,600,000
Land-Citrus Groves—De Soto County	23680	$2,960,000	Developed Orange Groves and Sold	$47,360,000
Land-Mercer Ranch—De Soto County	20000	$4,000,000	Sold to Florida Power & Light	$12,000,000

Property	Acres	Purchase Price	Status	Sale Value
Land-Riverfront—Nocatee—De Soto County	3600	$400,000	Partially Developed- Sold Back to Seller	$400,000
Highway Frontage—US#41—Charlotte County	85	$12,000	Holding for Sale	$2,550,000
Farm Land—Glades County	23040	$1,728,000	Sold in Acreage Tracts, etc.	$17,280,000
Land-De Soto County	640	$320,000	Developed in Orange Grove	$5,500,000
Land-Speculation- Charlotte County—Frontage on I-75	80	$80,000	Sold to Shopping Ctr Developer	$2,500,000
Beautiful Island—Lee County	44	$30,000	Holding for Sale	Uncertain Value
Pistachio Land—Fresno, California	3,000	$3,000,000	Planted Pistachio Groves	Grove value is substantially more than land
Citrus Grove—Hendry County	640	320,000	Sold	$3,000,000

TOTALS PURCHASED   88,789 acres = 139 square miles.

* This Schedule includes all properties purchased by the author for his companies and himself. Some of the properties were developed and sold; some are in the process of being sold or held for investment.

** These figures represent the gross sales of properties that were sold. On properties still unsold, the estimated sales value is displayed. On properties that were developed and sold as orange groves, lots, or acreage tracts, large funds were expended for development work, labor, materials, road work, marketing, and overhead.

CHAPTER FOURTEEN

HOW TO MAKE A FORTUNE IN

FLORIDA REAL ESTATE

L and is one of the foremost bases of wealth. While there are many facets of real estate investments, purchases, and sales, my career was centered exclusively in the area of land purchases, either for development or investment. Although I did purchase some land in Tennessee and California, my expertise was almost entirely in Florida properties.

In this final chapter I will explain how to cash in on the development of any area in the world where there is aggressive growth and a desirable living pattern. Although the real estate business has many facets, I will focus on only one aspect, the development of land into saleable parcels. It is a business that, besides being creative, can be very lucrative. Furthermore, there is a feeling of accomplishment when you see raw land converted into usable parcels, people building homes, farmers producing crops, weed-filled lots turning into lush gardens, and landscaped yards replacing random growth.

To proceed into the process as a developer or investor in land acquisition, the buyer must have certain personal qualifications. Not everyone can succeed. An "investor-developer" must possess the following capabilities:

1. An average amount of intelligence.
2. A bit of financial acumen.
3. Ability to think progressively.

4. A workable plan.
5. A reasonable amount of funds.
6. A bit of a gambling streak.
7. Ability to make decisions.
8. A "hunger" to succeed

So our erstwhile developer who possesses these attributes must now proceed to make his fortune. I shall set forth the road map to success, and list the varied items that must be considered by the neophyte developer. The same principles apply all over the globe.

1. *Select the Area and Growth Pattern:* Do not waste time or money on an area of declining or no growth. Do not try to reinvent the wheel! Go where people want to go. Consider all factors: climate, access to employment, people-friendly population, etc. Get all government statistics on population, growth pattern, etc. In the U.S. pick a state and area with rapid growth rate.

2. *Remember "Location, Location, Location."* The basic tenet of real estate acquisition is always location.

3. *Look for potential customers.* Remember this most important message:. "No tickee, no washee." No customers, no sales! Furthermore, decide the most desirable usage for your property purchase and what alternative usages are available if primary usage is not achieved.

4. *Develop a plan.* Know the procedures necessary to develop the property, the cost of development, the taxes, the cost of carrying the land, the marketing program, etc.

5. *Buy Road Frontage.* Property with road frontage on a state or federal highway can be a tremendous selling feature. If a property does not have this particular access, it is most important to have some available road access.

6. *Look for Waterfront Property.* One of the most profitable and best selling features is waterfront property. This is especially true in Florida. This state is blessed with many

hundred miles of ocean access, both on the Atlantic Ocean and on the Gulf of Mexico. Moreover, there are many rivers and streams that have access to the ocean or gulf. The value of waterfront property increases astronomically in marketing terms. I much prefer waterfront that is accessible to the ocean or gulf, since that permits a person with a boat unlimited water travel, virtually all over the world. However, there are hundreds of lakes in Florida and lakefront property has increased value over property not on water.

7. *Review Governmental Regulations:* Beware! Beware! Check all zoning and environmental regulations, Federal, State, County, and City. In the past thirty years, various governmental agencies have piled on regulations and obstacles to the development of land; most without apparent reason and certainly with no reasonable purpose. However, the developer must go through all of these government agencies to obtain a final development order.

8. *Be Aware of Environmental Regulations:* Unfortunately, many environmental groups have arisen in the past years. These people are destructive of all good progress. They also demand their "pound of flesh" and will hold up development, even after government approves it. Environmentalists use "mafia tactics" to extort funds from the developers for various noble sounding projects, but which have no real value. Meanwhile they fill their coffers with funds to fight all development. Their avowed purpose is to stop all progress.

I have described the many factors to consider in selecting the land to be purchased. Here are some of the items to consider in structuring the transaction:

1. *Options:* Another real estate truism is "Always take an option, never give an option." So when you are negotiating for property, try to get an option for the longest time

possible: 30 days, 90 days, 120 days, or one year. You may have to put up a deposit to obtain the option. Try to get a refundable deposit. If you have to pay for the option, make sure that it will give you sufficient time to close. Often you may be able to resell the property before closing and walk off with a profit.

2. *No Partners:* I personally refuse to buy property with a partner or partners, even if they are friends or relatives. Partners can cause trouble. They can abort the use or sale of property. Also remember that when you buy land with a partner, you automatically adopt his family, his heirs, and his economic and marital structure. If you conclude a deal requiring the partner's signature, he may refuse to sign; or his children, wife or friends may not permit him to sign. He may be going through a divorce, etc. Even if you set up a corporation or other entity, you still can't avoid partner trouble and litigation.

3. *Avoiding Partner Problems:* Eliminate partners. If you need financing, borrow from a bank or financial institution. Another device I have often used is physically splitting the property into several pieces with each partner receiving his pro-rata share.

4. *Financing:* It is usually possible to get owner financing from the seller. Try to get the best terms: the lowest down payment, the longest terms on the mortgage, the lowest possible interest rate. Use your powers of charm to arrange the best possible financial deal.

5. *Releases:* Negotiate the best possible releases from the mortgage. With each payment, you should get property released from the mortgage.

6. *Exit Strategy:* Always have an exit strategy. Determine your plan in the event of a worst-case scenario. Figure the best way to bail out. If you have a valid plan, you may not have a problem. However the possibility of needing to reverse course should be considered before the deal is consummated.

7. *Greed:* Some say greed is good. I say greed is bad. In fact, it is terrible! Greed could destroy the value and possibility of achieving a profitable deal. When you are in a transaction, you should decide the result you wish to attain. Establish a reasonable sales price, one that gives you a fair and reasonable profit. Negotiate up or down on price; however, do not be greedy. When you have negotiated the top possible price, do not lose the customer if you can make a reasonable deal. Many profitable sales are lost due to the seller's greed. When the buyer leaves town, the train has left the station. There is only one time that "Greed is Good." That occurs when the property is under condemnation by the government. I will explain later.

8. *Timing:* This is probably the most important factor in the sale of real estate. Unfortunately, no one person has control over this phenomenon. It is purely a "luck" factor. "Sometimes you are hot and sometimes your are not." However, being aware of national economic trends, stock market activity (which gauges the emotional attitudes of investors), and other macro-economic factors will assist in the judgment of timing.

Another important factor should be discussed at this point. It is called "condemnation." Often a governmental agency requires property from a landowner, either to build roads, construct a government facility or meet some government requirement. By law, a government has the legal right to "take" a person's property by "condemnation," if it serves a valid government need.

In the past, most condemnations were obtained for the building of roads. However, increasingly, government is taking private property for use of public facilities and for purposes that are not sanctioned by the United State Constitution. Unfortunately, in some cases, the courts have permitted the government to "take" land in violation of the Constitutional mandate.

Having had considerable experience with condemnations, I

can explain the procedures and the pitfalls. As previously stated, Greed is Bad. However, when it comes to condemnation, Greed is Good. When you are dealing at arm's length in a regular transaction, you have alternatives. You can use the tools of negotiation. There is a play and counter play between the parties. Thus, if the seller uses an excess of greed, he might lose the transaction. In condemnation, the result is already determined: the government gets the property. The seller has already lost the property! There is no other buyer available, no way that can change the outcome. The seller must get the best possible deal from the government since there is no alternative buyer with whom to negotiate.

Here are some of my experiences with condemnations:

In 1954, I was developing San Carlos Park. At that time, it was raw land, located on old U.S.#41, south of Ft. Myers. The government decided to four-lane the existing road and condemned about 2,000 feet of the property fronting on the highway. I had just moved to Florida and was naïve concerning condemnation procedures. I decided to donate this valuable property to the federal government because it would add more value to my existing land. It was a fine gesture. I called the government man in charge of the condemnation, and informed him of my desire to donate the property, dispensing with the legal formalities. He insisted that there had to be some money exchanged, so we set a very low price. The government was pleased, and I felt good about practically giving the property away. It was the right, patriotic thing to do! In a few days, the local newspaper became aware of this transaction. They blasted me for making a deal (under the table) with the government. Again, the reporter, unaware of the true nature of the transaction, made false accusations. I learned, then and there, that the government was always an adverse party in negotiations and should be regarded accordingly.

In condemnations, it is important to note that the government pays all the seller's costs. I have previously related the condemnation situation that I was involved in on the property in Punta Gorda. In that case, the government took 50 of the 80 acres for the building of I-75 and a rest area. When we could not negotiate a fair price, I went to court. I settled when the government offered a substantial price. I settled, because going before a jury might have presented other problems.

In another case, the government condemned some property in Lee County for the construction of I-75. The property was split in two by the highway right-of-way, which cut off all road access to one side of the property. In this event, the government must pay to build a road to the property that has been cut off due to the "taking." Usually the government pays a large sum to provide a road to the affected parcel. It was my understanding that the government always made a cash settlement in these cases. However, in this case, the government decided it would be cheaper to build the road to the parcel that was cut off. So they built a one and one-half mile road that we named Treeline Avenue. It will be one of the main roads in Lee County, Florida. It cost the government a large sum of money, but they paid much less for the property than they usually did.

I was fortunate to develop all my properties at a time before the government and the Environmental Movement became powerful. Every right-thinking person is a natural environmentalist. If a developer does not create a development in tune with the environment, he can't sell his product, whether it is a lot, property, or building. However, the Environmental Movement has now become an enormously powerful political force. It has refined the old Mafia tradition of blackmailing landowners and developers with outrageous and unwarranted payments, under threat of lawsuits. A new tactic that this movement has fine-tuned is lawsuits against government agencies, such as the Army Corps of Engineers and the Fish and Wildlife Agency, etc. to get the government to accede to their demands. Inevitably, the government agency backs off to avoid controversy and lawsuits.

The government itself, ruled by the game of politics, has become a major bottleneck to progress. The constitutional guarantee of the right to private property ownership is being violated not only by the agencies of government but, increasingly, by the courts. Thus, vocal and organized groups work the political process to undermine the individual liberties we so prize in this country.

For example, the Nature Conservancy is a group that purchases or receives gifts of land supposedly to be held in a natural condition. However, in a series of articles in the *Washington Post*, the newspaper disclosed that the Nature Conservancy has sold some of these pristine lands to its trustees at a discount for fabulous private-home sites. The Nature Conservancy has three billion dollars in assets and took in approximately $721 million in annual revenue in 2001. This is hardly a pristine natural conservatory! Sounds like big business to me! The Nature Conservancy receives millions of dollars in oil and gas revenues on land that it acquired to protect native birds; however it allows oil and gas development on that property. While it publicly protests that it is against the cutting of forestlands, it leases land to timber companies for that purpose. And this is only one environmental group. There are many others.

Every situation has both a good and a bad result. The bad results of "environmentalism" and the resultant political government response are not obvious, but they are nevertheless very real and very costly. They have driven the price of property and homeownership costs to unprecedented heights! Since it takes a developer usually more than three years to acquire approval for land to build homes, the costs spiral up astronomically. The developer needs a full staff of architects, engineers, environmental consultants, and staff engineers. He needs approvals from over thirty government agencies—national, state, and local—before he can begin his project. When he has finally received all his approvals after many years, then the environmental vultures descend and demand their "pound of flesh," threatening to sue and hold up development. They demand money to buy land for an endangered panther, or a turtle, or a bird, or an eagle. The environmentalists always get their blackmail. The developer cannot afford the time for lawsuits. He pays the blackmail. When the project finally gets underway after three or four years, the unwitting homebuyer or lot buyer does not understand that 50% to 75% of the cost of the project is due to nonsensical government ideas or to the environmental vultures. The homeowner pays through the nose! The government is increasingly embracing a system of full disclosure, in food labeling, for example. Don't you think that the citizen consumer and homebuyer should be entitled to the same disclosure? He should know the exorbitant cost that he is being charged for ill-advised environmental and governmental policies.

Now for the good news! The governmental and environmental costs have driven the cost of development to new heights. These costs not only have limited the usage of property, but also the amount of property that can be developed. Thus the owner of property that is for sale to a developer or builder can, and does, demand a high price for his property for many reasons. First of all, he may receive a deposit to hold the land pending the three-year approval process, but he cannot close or receive his money until part of the approval process is underway. Secondly, the quantity of land available has diminished because of government and environmentalist "takings." There are always turtles, panthers, and insects that need land for preservation. So save the insects and kill the people! Therefore the seller can and does command a much higher price for the diminished available land. It is thus ironic that the environmentalists, who are anti-developer and anti-property owners are actually assisting property owners and developers to achieve greater profits for their labor, all at the cost of the unknowing consumer!

It is important for the potential real estate investor, speculator, or developer to be fully aware of the positive and negative factors that are outlined here. The process of providing properties and homes to the citizens of this country is very important.

Politically motivated groups should not thwart the process!

EPILOGUE

Because my book focuses on business and entrepreneurship, I didn't include much personal information. However, since I owe part of my success to the support and cooperation of my wonderful family, I want to give them special thanks for all they are and what they have accomplished.

In Chapter Two I have already mentioned my hard-working parents, who emigrated from Poland in the 1900's. Their good business sense and ambition were models that I have followed all my life. Because my brother Jules was an integral part of my entrepreneurial experiences, he also appears in several chapters of the book. He has been an inspiration to me throughout our lives.

My beloved sister Sylvia nurtured me as a child and has continued to help my family and me whenever we needed her. She and her husband Louis were valued employees of our company—unsurpassed in establishing and maintaining good relationships with our customers and residents.

Of course my beautiful wife Gertrude has been a mainstay in my life. During our sixty-two years of marriage, she has put up with my foibles and taken care of our family's needs and desires. And she has done so with class and grace. When we lived in Coral Gables, Gertrude went back to college, attended the University of Miami and, upon graduation, received a Bachelor of Arts degree. Because of her education, artistic knowledge and talent, Gertrude was involved in art and museum activity in South Florida, represented several artists and sculptors as an agent, and has amassed a fine collection of antiques and artistic works.

The oldest of our children, Mark, is an artist, an architect, and a successful developer. He lives in Ft. Myers and, while his first love is art and painting, he has developed a model residential community on Pine Island, Florida. In addition, he has completed several industrial park projects and is still planning and working on additional developments on the west coast of Florida. Mark attended the University of Florida in Gainesville and received a degree in Architecture. While at the university, because of his artistic ability, he became the cartoonist for the college newspaper, the *"Alligator."* Upon graduation, he went to work in New York for a large architectural company. When I was President of American Agronomics Co., and we were developing several community projects, including San Carlos Park, I asked Mark to return to Florida and work for our company. Over a period of a few months, Mark successfully had the entire San Carlos Park development zoned and approved by the county and other governmental agencies. This was truly an amazing feat, and was largely instrumental in the success of our community, which today is home to approximately 25,000 people. When we were building a golf course at San Carlos, at my request, Mark designed and constructed the Club House. Because he wanted the freedom to start his own enterprise, he decided to leave the company. However, Mark is happiest as he transforms a large blank canvas into an artistic masterpiece. He has been painting and sketching from the time he was a small child; now as a competent artist, Mark captures the foibles of mankind in humorous paintings of today's society.

Our middle son Jeffrey is an excellent businessman, with a natural talent for structuring deals and motivating people to accomplish his programs. He is one of the best marketing people I have ever met. He has been my prime salesperson to put together and sell the thousands of acres for our business and private accounts. Jeffrey is a people-person. As a boy of ten, he would open a small stand on a highway, selling whatever fruit was in season. Unbeknownst to his parents, he also had a lucrative business selling candy to the kids at school. In fact, the candy business was so good, that he employed several other kids as assistants. Thankfully, this was while young boys and girls were still buying candy instead of illicit substances! Jeffrey attended the University of Miami, but after two years, he tired of school and sought other goals. Our company had built a motel at San Carlos Park that was losing money. We put Jeffrey in charge. He rearranged some rooms, set up a game room for young people, and revised the restaurant menu. In a few months, the motel turned profitable. My brother Jules was in charge of the marketing program and when Jeff complained that the sales office was totally out of sync, Jules asked Jeff, who was all of twenty-one years old, whether he could do better. Jeff said he would take the job as Sales Manager with zero salary, on the condition that he is compensated if he generated sales above a certain volume. This was very fair to the company, so Jeff was hired, and he initiated all kinds of sales promotions. Besides opening a free orange juice stand on the highway to entice prospects to visit the development, he set up an airlift from various Florida beach resorts to fly tourist prospects to visit the property. Jeffrey had the natural talent and ability necessary to become a success on his own, so at my urging, he left the company to start his own real estate business. Besides building a successful real estate business, he has accumulated a sizeable, valuable land portfolio.

After having a good meal, a sweet dessert is a necessary ingredient. After Gertrude and I had two sons, we wanted a girl to complete our family. We were certainly blessed when Helene arrived. She is a joy to her parents and countless friends. Helene attended the University of South Florida, received a degree in marketing and went to work for Arvida Real Estate. After a few years, they promoted her to Marketing Director of their Orange Tree Development in Orlando, where she completed the sale of a 500 home development. Her first son, Aaron was born soon after that and Helene opted to be a mother and homemaker. She has been married to David, for over 20 years. David is a wonderful husband and son-in-law. He is a developer and banker, and he and Helene have three boys, Aaron, Jason and Michael who are a joy to parents, grandparents, and friends.

Gertrude and I are blessed with six grandchildren and one great grandchild. Mark's daughter Heather has been an equestrian since childhood. She has won many trophies in this field and has been teaching the art of horsemanship for years to both children and adults. Heather met Michael at college and married this fellow, who, believe it or not, is a "rocket scientist." He has several degrees in science and engineering, and works on developing new and better electronic "mouse traps" for the government.

Son Jeffrey is married to Risa, a delightful daughter-in-law. They have two children, Brian and Jill. Brian, a successful attorney, is married to Suzette and they live in Ft. Myers in a wonderful old stone house built in the 1930's. Jill and her husband Scott, a businessman, have produced our first great granddaughter, Morgan.

Daughter Helene and son-in-law David have given us three grandsons, Aaron, Jason and Michael. Michael is eleven and Aaron and Jason are teenagers. They all are good students but also into all forms of athletics. They attend private school in the Orlando area. Helene is a dedicated soccer mom so she and David are constantly transporting the three boys to soccer, football and basketball games. All the boys are on their school teams, but in addition to their athletic schedules, both parents make sure that the students do their homework and chores.

I believe that the description of our family stories and relationships is a fitting conclusion to this book. My greatest success has been in establishing and maintaining family relationships.